Would all of Emily's dreams go up in smoke?

Stumbling and tripping, she ran across the field with a shovel in one hand and a wet rag to tie across her face in the other, sending up incoherent pleas to God, the firemen, Simon, and anyone else she could think of who might help. There was no way she could put out a fire alone, even though she was determined to try.

Sometime later she heard the keening of the fire engines, but she was too busy to be relieved. Smoke stung her eyes and burned her nose, heat scorched and blistered her face and hands as she dug into the earth and flung heavy shovelfuls over the flames. She was much too preoccupied to notice a sinister figure creeping stealthily out from the woods behind her.

The blow caught her at the back of her neck. She went down like a pine sapling felled by a single swipe of the ax. When the fire engines pulled up five minutes later, there was no sign of Emily.

SARA MITCHELL is the author of five books. In addition to her novel writing, Mitchell has also authored several musical dramas.

Restore The Joy

Sara Mitchell

Sara Mitchell
Isa. 40:31

Heartsong Presents

ISBN 1-55748-324-8

RESTORE THE JOY

PRINTED IN U.S.A.

Prologue

Death was lurking in the room. Lying in a huge tester bed, a man breathed in labored gasps, his complexion beneath the full black beard and mustache waxen, the flesh clammy. His eyes opened and fixed upon a weeping woman sitting beside him.

"Do you understand?" he repeated hoarsely, with great effort. "Do you understand why I had to do it this way?"

The woman fingered the lace of her cashmere breakfast jacket, then reached and laid her trembling hand over his where it lay clutching the bedclothes. "I understand, Everett," she murmured in a tearful voice. "Please try not to tire yourself now." Her voice caught, and she turned her head aside so the man would be spared the sight of her stricken face.

She was a lovely woman, with rich black hair gathered in a bun on top of her head and fashionably fuzzy ringlets framing her face. But deep unhappiness and shame had left their marks. She had had to pay a heavy price to be with this man, and she knew that, as he prepared himself to meet his Maker, he was trying to atone for both their sins.

"You...and Harold...will be...comfortable," he was gasping out now, his breathing even more labored. "Won't have to worry about yourself...or our son."

"Thank you," the woman whispered humbly. He might have built her this mansion and showered her with material possessions, but she had always known of his feelings of guilt.

"Must do what's fair, what's right." For a minute he rested, gathering the strength to finish. "I can't rest in peace...through eternity...with the VanCleef name tarnished. This—this will help restore honor...to rightful...heirs."

His chest rose heavily and fell, and his eyes closed so he did not see the fresh pain washing into the woman's face. Suddenly he roused and with surprising strength gripped her hand. "But I did love you, Gwinette...." His parched lips parted in a smile and the unfocussed eyes assumed a satisfied, faraway cast. "Got you the window like I promised, didn't I?"

"Yes, Everett, you got me my beautiful Tiffany window. And I love you for it." Tears crowded her throat and she stopped, her heart breaking.

"Only one other window like that...." His eyes dimmed now, and the strength went out of his grip. "It's still there, I imagine....I wonder...if she ever forgave me...." The words died away, and his hand slipped from her fingers to the heavy silk counterpane.

He died an hour later, and the sober attending physician laid the covers over his head and put a comforting hand on the woman's shoulder. She waited until the doctor left the room, then walked slowly around the bed to pick up a document lying on a table. Carefully and quietly, she found the safety deposit box Everett had kept hidden in the secret place at the back of the closet.

It would be so easy to destroy the document, to tell the lawyer Everett had changed his mind and dictated a new one to her. But she couldn't. She had given herself to Everett, thereby blighting her reputation and his, so she could not destroy his feeble effort to redeem himself.

She had this house—with the window she had coveted from the moment she saw its twin at his home in New York—and she had their son. Everett had been as faithful to her as he knew how to be. In the end, though, it hadn't been enough. Man's faithfulness alone never is.

one

Dear Emily,

Just thought we'd drop a line and let you know we've made it as far as Virginia. Beautiful scenery—it's great having all this freedom to go and come as we please. Keep the home fires burning. Love, Mom and Dad.

What home fires? Emily Carson thought with resigned humor as she read the postcard from her parents. The little square frame house she had lived in all her life had been sold three months before. In its place, Dad had purchased a monolith motor home, complete with every luxurious appointment known to man. He and Mom had kissed Emily goodbye, asked her to maintain contact with her younger brother Jimmy-Joe, and taken off for parts unknown.

Emily dropped the postcard in the round straw basket she had purchased to hold the sporadic remembrances from her mother. Let's see—today's note made three, so that was about one a month. She sighed.

It was a hot, lazy day in early June. School had just been released, with shouts of freedom from the students and gasps of relief from the teachers. Emily Carson was a teacher, only she had not gasped in relief. She missed her kids already because for the past five years it was from them—and them alone—that she drew meaning and purpose for her life.

A plain, quiet girl with straight nut brown hair and

solemn brown eyes, Emily had learned early in life to combat her poor self-image and lack of popularity by working as hard and as long as she could. Gainfully employed since the age of fifteen, she had opened her own bank account when she started college. Now at twenty-six, she had—thanks to her parents' radical lifestyle transformation—her own apartment, a compact car, and an overwhelming sense of loneliness.

The loneliness was harder to ward off in the summer months, so Emily had taken to driving around the south Georgia countryside since school let out the previous week. She never drove with a destination in mind; if a road looked inviting, she simply turned and followed it. Narrow country lanes of packed clay or sand crisscrossed paved county roads, which intersected the larger state highways she invariably left to follow those other winding, bumpy lanes and roads. Eventually she would happen onto a signpost, and when she was ready, she'd wander back toward Sylvan, the sleepy, slow-moving town where she had lived all her life.

Today her beat up Toyota headed east, where forests of pine, fields of corn, soybeans, and tobacco, tumble-down shacks, and one-corner communities all blurred together as the miles ticked away on the odometer of the car. She would have missed the house outside Timmons altogether if it hadn't been for rays of sunlight striking off one of its windows directly onto Emily's windshield. Wincing, Emily glanced over to the right to see what had caused the sudden glare and caught her breath. The car swerved as she jammed the brakes, then backed up with careless haste and stopped dead in the middle of the ancient dirt road upon which she had been traveling.

Half hidden by towering oaks and elms, almost strangled by overgrown azaleas, rhododendrons, and a healthy crop of weeds, a house straight out of nineteenth century Victorian America resided in faded splendor right there before Emily's incredulous eyes. In that first astonishing moment of discovery, all she saw was that the two story structure was constructed—incredibly for south Georgia—entirely of brick. Then, as her delighted eyes moved over the gables and steeply pitched slate roof and the wooden gingerbread porches, her gaze fell at last on the huge bay window. In spite of the accumulation of dust and dirt and years of neglect, the sunbeams had found this diamond in the rough and offered it to her—plain old Emily Carson.

She had never seen a window quite like this one. She had never seen a *house* quite like this one. With careful but eager movements, she stepped across a ditch and picked her way through beggar's lice and tall scratchy grasses and a multitude of other undesirable weeds to stand in front of the bay window.

The side panels were of clear beveled glass panes. Matching smaller panes created a frame for the center panel, which was of leaded glass. Emily reached trembling fingers and gently smoothed away some of the layers of grime. A shimmering, soft shade of luminous lemon-gold appeared.

Clumsy with excitement, she used the hem of her shirt to clean a larger space, and a minute later her eyes confirmed what her brain refused to believe: the front panel of leaded glass depicted an intricate floral pattern complete with leaves and branches intertwined in glorious, richly hued colors. Lips parted, breathing suspended, Emily stared at this vision of delight with the growing seed of an idea clamoring to take root.

She wanted this house. More than anything else on this earth, she wanted this house. She wanted to restore it, uncover all its dignity and charm and elegance, resurrect this huge, decaying ghost from out of the past and give meaning and purpose to her own life as well. She would live here and become something beyond plain old Emily Carson, abandoned and rootless. She *needed* this house. This house needed *her*.

An unfamiliar, tantalizing emotion bubbled up and through her. She stood a moment longer, staring at the house, hands clasped to her chest as if to keep her heart from bursting through. Then she whirled, scrambled into her car, and tore off down the dirt lane with unladylike haste.

Over the next weeks Emily Carson acquired three things. The first was an alarmingly large dog whom she dubbed Ivan the Terrible. Ivan had just passed his first birthday and was housebroken. The second was a scruffy, flea-riddled kitten. Two former students begged Emily to save the animal from its dismal, but certain, fate. Her third acquisition was the house.

Upon closer inspection of the latter, Emily learned that the room with the beautiful bay window must have been a library. Floor-to-ceiling shelves on two walls, empty now of books and coated with dust and dead insects, clued her to this snippet of information.

Upstairs, she also discovered traces of former residents—someone who must have camped out in a couple of the rooms for awhile. Emily stuffed empty beer cans and filthy litter into a sack and stomped angrily downstairs. If any wandering hoboes made a return visit, she'd toss them out on their ears. This was *her* house now.

She planned to restore it one room at a time as finances

permitted. The library would be first—except for her hidden treasure of a window. That jewel she would save for last.

Where had it come from? She had seen stained glass windows before, but only in churches, and even those did not resemble the one here. And it was hers now. Hers to savor, hers to dream over and wonder about its past.

By the middle of July, Emily was sanding down the mantel over the fireplace with the belt sander a man at the Timmons hardware store had recommended. The wood, she was told, was mahogany, although the bookshelves and molding were oak. Fingers now as red and rough as the sandpaper on the tool she was using, Emily nonetheless delighted in each new discovery she made about her new home. Solid oak floors, five fireplaces including one in the kitchen, large airy rooms fringed with intricate crown molding and filled with sunlight—every day she stumbled onto a bonus she was sure had to be the last.

Buying the house may have taken almost every penny in her savings account, but it was worth it. It was doubly worth it considering the weeks of trouble and uncertainty and tedious searching and waiting before this glorious palace was hers...all hers.

Emily rubbed her hands hard against the small of her back, sitting on her heels to rest a minute as her mind idly mulled over the past hectic month. If it hadn't been for a nice, but nosy, old man shamelessly eavesdropping in the county courthouse that day—

From outside came the sound of a car door slamming, and Emily twisted her head. What on earth? She wasn't expecting the electrician until tomorrow. He had checked and repaired the existing wiring already, but Emily wanted some new outlets, and he had promised to drop by in the morning.

"Anybody home?" a man's voice called out a moment later, and Emily stood up with a sigh. She might have known it! This was probably one of those disgusting vagrants who made free with other people's property. Well, he had a surprise in store.

"In here," she answered grimly, rising to her full five feet six inches and preparing to intimidate with her best stern schoolteacher's demeanor. She shoved a few straggling locks of hair out of her face, then froze.

Like Emily, the man was wearing jeans, but his weren't covered with sawdust. A shaft of sunlight glinted off sandy brown hair, revealing deep chestnut highlights among the rebellious waves spilling haphazardly about his face. Although he obviously tried to control his hair by keeping it cropped about the ears and neck, the first impression was quite dramatic. To Emily, he resembled the statue of an ancient Greek.

His eyes, warm and a startling shade of green, were amused. Emily realized with a start that she was staring. "I'm sorry," she apologized, and grinned sheepishly. "I wasn't expecting anyone—especially someone who looks like you."

"Someone who looks like me?" the stranger repeated with a charming, white-toothed grin. "What does that mean, or should I ask?"

Emily laughed. "Oh, nothing special, I assure you. My first thought was that you were one of the bums who had used my home for a pit stop some time in the past." She tilted her head to one side and studied him. "But somehow I don't think you're a bum... and you're definitely an improvement over the plumber. He was about fifty years old and that many pounds overweight.

The termite man was just the opposite—in his twenties and skinny as a maple sapling. He also chewed tobacco."

As she talked, she ticked the numbers off on her fingers, enjoying the frank appreciation of the man's response without analyzing why she felt so free to tease. "The roofing man wasn't too bad, but he had a wife and four kids. He showed me their pictures."

"Well, I'm not married, I'm thirty-three, and I don't chew tobacco. And I'm definitely not a homeless vagrant."

"You're not overweight either," Emily couldn't help adding, and they both laughed.

The stranger began prowling slowly about the room, eyeing it with entirely too much interest to suit Emily. Stroking the mantel with a proprietary hand, she watched him with the wariness of a mother dog defending her pups. He ran a finger along a section of the molding she had sanded down, then knelt suddenly to examine the tongue-in-groove hardwood floors.

"What *did* you want?" Emily prodded, his easy silence making her somehow nervous.

The man dusted his hands and turned back to her. For a minute he studied her in silence, then remarked casually, "I understand you've bought this old place. Is that correct?"

"Yes." Emily stared back, her own gaze speculative. "How did you find out—and why do you want to know?"

"I asked in Timmons. Apparently you've generated more business—and gossip—than they've enjoyed in a decade or more."

He sounded half-amused, half-bemused, and in some confusion Emily turned and picked up the belt sander from the mantelpiece. "Everyone has been...mostly helpful. Look, I don't want to be rude but I am busy, as you can see. If you're trying to sell insurance or something, you're wasting your time. I've spent every dime I have in the world on this place, and every dime I hope to make in the future as well."

"I'm not an insurance salesman." He paused, then added, "But you do need adequate, specialized insurance on a place like this. It's financial suicide not to."

"I'm not stupid," Emily replied stiffly. "It's insured. Now if you don't mind...who are you and would you please hurry up and go?"

One thick sable eyebrow shot up, and a chuckle echoed deep in his throat. "Yes, ma'am!" His gaze wandered over the room again, ending with another examination of Emily. A strange expression flitted through his eyes, but his voice remained pleasantly bland. "The realtor—a Mrs. Davis, I believe—told me you were doing most of the work yourself."

Emily's chin lifted. "Yes, I am."

"You've taken on an overwhelming project, you know. Do you have any idea what you're demanding of yourself to try and do it alone?" He hesitated, then spoke as if choosing his words with more than usual care. "There are businesses devoted to this kind of work, and it seems like it would be prudent to take advantage of their expertise. As a matter of fact—"

"All they would do is take advantage of my pocketbook," Emily retorted. "Besides, I *want* to do it myself." She waved her hand with the sander in it. "I don't think I've done too badly for a rank beginner in home restoration." She flashed him a determined grin. "I realize I jumped in the deep end before I learned more than a dog-paddle, but I'm not a klutz. Besides, I couldn't afford to hire someone who had to be paid to do what I'm doing for free. I told you it took every penny I had to buy the place."

Her own gaze roved fondly about the room, ending on the window—her pot of gold, the reward for the hours and days and weeks of labor. She was saving the window to do last because the anticipation of what it would look like kept her going long after her body begged for rest. "But it's worth it," she whispered almost to herself. "Oh, it's worth it."

She abruptly became aware that the stranger was watching her with a peculiar expression, his body poised in an attitude of unnatural stillness. Coloring a little, she started to change the subject, but even as she opened her mouth, he moved, walking in swift sure strides across to her window.

"What's this?"

There was sufficient excitement in his voice for Emily to become alarmed. She didn't want to share her window with anybody. It was her secret, and no one else—especially some nosy stranger—was going to poke around and discover what lay beneath the concealing layers of grime.

"It's a window," she understated.

The man tossed an impatient glance over his shoulder. "It's more than just a window, and I think you know it."

He reached into his hip pocket and withdrew a neatly folded white handkerchief. Before Emily could reach him, he had carefully cleaned off a six-inch square, revealing a deep, wine-colored rosebud. Inhaling sharply, he muttered something Emily didn't catch because she was too busy scurrying over and grabbing his arm. "Leave it alone!" she snapped, too desperate to be polite. Her fingers dug into a forearm covered with soft, curling brown hair, but the muscles beneath were as hard and unyielding as the oak bannister out in the hall.

His hand came up and very gently covered hers. "I'm not going to hurt your window." He withdrew his hand and moved away. "It is yours, I take it? According to the realtor you paid cash and closed the deal as fast as the reports came in attesting to the basic soundness of the place."

"Yes. It's mine," Emily stated flatly. "I found it and spent a week unearthing as much as I could of its history at the county courthouse. I found the real estate company who handled it, and they sold it to me. I'm going to restore it and turn it back into the thing of beauty it used to be, and no one is going to stop me."

Her impassioned speech rang into the hot stillness of the day, and she stared up into the stranger's impassive face with her own feelings shamelessly exposed.

"You feel pretty strongly about it, don't you?" he commented after a moment, his voice and green eyes suddenly softening.

"Yes," said Emily. "I do." She was amazed at how much she was letting a perfect stranger see, but she sensed on a subconscious level that he posed a threat of some kind. Perhaps if he were convinced of her dedication and determination, he would go away and leave her alone.

"About five months ago my parents up and sold the only home I've ever known," Emily explained. "They bought themselves one of those mile long motor homes and took off for the wild blue yonder. My brother joined the Air Force. He just shipped out to Germany, and I probably won't see him for three years."

Hands planted on her hips, head held high, she stared the man straight in the eye. "This house is all I have in this world that means something to me besides the dog and cat that got dumped on me a month ago. I need it—and it needs me. So, I don't know who you are or what you want, but if it has to do with this house, forget it. I'm not interested."

"My name is Simon Balfour, and I'm afraid I am here about the house, and I'll have to have your interest whether desired or not." His disconcerting green eyes probed hers briefly, but then, to Emily's amazement, Simon bowed his head and closed his eyes as if he were about to offer up a prayer.

For the first time Emily knew fear, and she found herself wanting to pray, too. Although she had come to an awareness of her need for God while in college, she had never felt the need to bother Him overmuch with the petty day to day details of her life. She had always felt the Lord had more important things on His mind than the niggling problems of Emily Carson. Right now, however, her problems loomed with the significance of the last trumpet call, and she found herself sending up a desperate plea for divine intervention in her behalf.

Simon Balfour opened his eyes and looked at her again, this time with pain—and pity. He turned abruptly away. "There's a title dispute," he declared without looking at Emily.

"Title dispute?" she echoed stupidly.

Simon turned back, his face a mask of frustration. "Yes," he confirmed harshly, then, as he watched the impact of his message register, his voice softened. "I'm sorry. If it's any consolation, I feel like I've just booted a baby bird out of its nest...from what you tell me of your parents."

"There can't be a dispute. It's legal. Mildred didn't say anything." She stared at him, so stunned she couldn't even take offense at what he had called her.

"Why don't we go sit outside on the steps, and I'll explain?" Simon suggested.

As they walked across the creaking, slightly sagging porch, Emily's shell-shocked gaze wandered over the wild beauty of the front yard. "Prove it," she demanded suddenly in an upsurge of sheer protectiveness. "Give me some proof of your allegation or I'll throw you off this property. My property, I might remind you."

"I don't have any proof with me right now," Simon admitted slowly, a spark of reluctant amusement lighting his face at her outrageous threat. "I came out here to meet you, introduce myself." Amusement spread as he surveyed Emily from the dust-streaked, frazzled braid unraveling down her back to the equally dust-streaked, frazzled sneakers on her feet. "Just to satisfy my curiosity, how would you go about throwing me off your property?"

Emily put two fingers to her lips and whistled with the easy expertise of a ten-year-old boy. In a minute, Ivan came bounding across the yard through the three-foot high weeds. One Sunday afternoon, Emily and her friend Barb had passed the time speculating on Ivan's ancestry. They stopped after Great Dane, German shepherd, collie, and Doberman pinscher, deciding the effort was fruitless and it was easier just to call the animal a gigantic mutt. His back came almost to Emily's waist; his face, almost shaped like that of a Great Dane, had the longer hair of a shepherd. He looked horribly ferocious and had a bark to send shivers down the spine of a sumo wrestler, but it was all show. He retained the gregarious personality of a puppy. Of course Simon Balfour didn't know that.

The man's eyes opened wide at the sight of the dog, who leaped up the steps and stopped short when he saw Simon. Ivan growled, then barked twice—his invitation to play. Emily stood with arms crossed and a smug expression on her face. She gave Simon Balfour credit, however, for although he looked uneasy, he didn't bolt.

"Nice dog," he intoned dryly, holding out his palm for Ivan to sniff.

"Sometimes," Emily murmured back provokingly. Ivan turned from licking Simon's hand to whining playfully around Emily's feet, acting about as threatening now as he actually was. When Emily's eyes met Simon's again, she smiled reluctantly. "Okay. So I couldn't throw you off the place, and my watchdog would welcome Genghis Khan if he offered to play catch first." She sat down abruptly, humor wilting as she shooed her pet away after failing to dodge his wet tongue. "Please. Don't lie to me. Tell me why you're here."

Ivan padded off with an injured air and collapsed with a loud sigh in the corner of the long porch. "I wouldn't lie to you, Emily Carson," Simon promised with quiet sincerity. "Or to anyone else, for that matter."

"How noble," Emily retorted with a touch of acerbity. "Everyone lies if it suits his purpose to do so."

"You don't have much faith in people, do you?"

Emily shrugged. "I suppose not. No one has ever given me much reason why I should."

"What about God? Can even He earn your trust?"

Emily jerked her head around, wondering if she had heard right. Was he joking, being sarcastic? He met her astonishment and wariness with a clear-eyed serenity that was either completely guileless or the product of years of polished acting. "I don't see where my views on God have anything to do with the situation here," she finally hedged. "Are you stalling or something?"

Simon gave a rueful laugh and sat up. "I was perfectly

serious in my question, but yeah—I was stalling." He paused. "I've discovered I have this tremendous aversion to hurting you. And I'm afraid, after talking with you these few minutes, that what I have to tell you is going to hurt you pretty badly. I've been praying ever since I saw what this place meant to you, if you want to know."

"The title dispute...." She spoke the words as if referring to a repugnant, noxious weed. "Are you trying to tell me you're claiming this as your house?"

"Not exactly." He stirred restlessly. Emily sat unmoving, her very stillness betraying a fear she didn't want to admit. "It's my great aunt, actually. She claims the house belongs to her by virtue of a will that—unfortunately—hasn't been found yet. The property was supposed to have been left in trust with the realtors you dealt with."

Emily shook her head, trying to understand. "My real estate agent never said a word. Mildred didn't know anything about the place other than referring to it as the old deCourier place like everyone else in Timmons. We searched for the deed together. She was just as excited as I was...." Emily's voice faltered. "It doesn't make any sense. In fact, I don't believe you." Bewilderment hardened to accusation. "You're just trying to take my house away from me so you can tear it down and build condominiums or something."

"No, I'm not." Simon's voice and face oozed compassion and regret, and Emily's suspicion faltered. "I don't understand about your realtor, although she did mention something about her mother being her partner, but away for a three-month Mediterranean cruise. Maybe *she* would have known."

He fingered the wilting blossoms of a huge, lavender hydrangea planted by the front porch steps decades before. "All I know is what I learned from Aunt Iris, who might be seventy-six years old but has the finesse of a Sherman tank. She called my mother about a month ago ranting and raving about someone snatching her inheritance out from under her."

His gaze wandered over the wild, overgrown yard, a reflective, somewhat calculating look on his face as if he were imagining what it would look like all cleaned up. "Apparently some old codger who lives around here mentioned the sale to his sister, who is a long-time acquaintance of Aunt Iris. The woman commented on the sale in a letter to my great aunt, who promptly declared war over it. Included in her campaign was a rather heated call to my mother—Iris's niece. Mother got hold of me and persuaded me to see if I could find out what was going on."

He sighed, and muttered in an undertone, "I don't know why she didn't call my brother Geoff, but I suppose due to the circumstances...." He raised his voice and smiled at Emily, who did not return the gesture.

"Aunt Iris is a little less than five feet high and weighs maybe ninety-five pounds. But she's Attila the Hun and Queen Victoria all wrapped up in one package, and it's sort of hard to refuse when she gets a bee in her bonnet." In spite of herself, a smile tugged at Emily's lips. He sounded like a little boy and resembled one at the moment, the way he was toying with the flowers and avoiding her eyes, talking about this great-aunt as if she were some monstrous dictator holding a gun to his head.

"Anyway," Simon continued, "Aunt Iris swears there is a will somewhere in this house that stipulates the place has to remain in our family for a hundred years from the date of the will."

"Is that legal?"

"I've talked to my brother, who is a lawyer. If the will is found and is a proper will, then yes, it's legal."

"Why didn't your brother take care of all this, then? Why did your great aunt want you to get involved?"

Simon heaved a bone-deep sigh, contemplated his jogging shoes, then faced Emily squarely. "She wanted me to find out the details so I could get rid of you before you did too much damage to the house. Aunt Iris wants it renovated as well, but she wants *me* to do it." He paused, then finished almost roughly, "You see, I'm a professional contractor, Emily, and head a company specializing in period home restoration."

two

Emily jumped to her feet, face white beneath the streaks of dirt and perspiration. "You won't *touch* my house! Not so much as pound a nail or paint a single board! Get out."

"Miss Carson—Emily—"

Panicked now, Emily ignored him. "There's no aunt, no will—you just heard about my house and want it for yourself!" Her voice rose. Ivan, hearing the unusual sound of his mistress yelling, rose and trotted over, nudging her with a damp inquisitive nose. Simon rose, too, and put his hand on Emily's arm. She knocked it away with a force that surprised both of them.

"Get him, Ivan!" she commanded the dog, her voice almost breaking now. "Attack, you stupid animal. He's trying to take away my house." Her gaze ricocheted around wildly, ending with Simon, who stood a little ways from her now, his eyes very green. The outburst died as abruptly as it had erupted, and Emily plopped back down on the top step, shoulders slumped in exhaustion and mortification. Ordinarily, she was not a demonstrative, passionate woman, one who wore her feelings on her sleeve. She had a reputation as an easy-going, absent-minded, tolerant creature with a heart like warm oatmeal. She never got angry, never lost her temper, and was frankly appalled to discover she *had* a temper.

But she had also never been as unnerved as she was at this moment.

Simon came down the steps and hunkered down in

front of her, balancing on the second step from the bottom with the ease of a gymnast. "I am truly sorry," he repeated quietly. "It's a mess, and we're just going to have to work together to find a way out of it."

"You and your family can work any way you please," Emily responded in a tight, cold voice. "Until you present me with an affidavit proving otherwise this is my property, my house. And I plan to keep on restoring it the way I please." She glared at Simon. "And you can tell your Attila the Hun of an aunt that just because it's your job and I haven't done it before, doesn't mean I can't restore *my* home just as well as you can."

Incredibly, Simon grinned. "So there," he finished for her, and stood up. "Well...I think I'll take myself off now, since you're obviously not interested in negotiation at the moment. Not," he added with a rueful sigh, "that I blame you." He started down the steps, then stopped, turning back. "There's an old hymn I love...it reminds me that God's eye watches over us all the time—"His Eye Is On the Sparrow"? I've been thinking about it the last few minutes, when I had to warn a sparrow that she might be kicked out of her nest."

He stared down at her a minute more, then loped off toward his car. Ivan bounded after him, leaping and running in circles and barking happily. Simon ignored the dog, but just before he climbed back inside his snappy little sports convertible, he looked across the yard at Emily one last time. She returned the look, refusing to move until he ducked into the car, started the engine, and drove away.

Emily had been working in the daytime at the house, then driving the thirty miles or so back to her apartment at night. After the confrontation with Simon Balfour, however, she determined to move in lock, stock, and barrel as fast as she could. Possession, after all, was nine-tenths of the law.

It took almost a week to transfer her belongings, during which time Emily also resigned her teaching position in Sylvan. She crammed most of her things into the dining room since she had no plans for entertaining until she finished restoring her new home. Her parents had told her she was welcome to the contents of the house they'd all lived in for over thirty years. Emily never let them know how much their attitude hurt. They discarded it all—as if everything had the sentimental value of a worn out shoe.

About like they discarded J.J. and me, Emily found herself thinking late one night. She kicked the crumpled sheet, rolled on one side and then the other, and finally fluffed her pillow so she could sit up and be miserable. And alone. Thanks to her best friend, she was acutely aware that she was a single woman, living alone.

Barb and Taylor Chakensis and their two children had helped her move, and Barb—a perpetual worrier—fretted over Emily. She made such a fuss over Emily's job situation, her isolation, and the possible re-appearance of Simon Balfour that Emily herself was becoming paranoid.

"Look," Emily had finally said, "I've applied in Timmons for a teaching position, and I should have the phone in a few more weeks. Until then, if a motorcycle gang from L.A. decide to camp out here, I'll feed 'em lunch." She ignored Barb's rolling eyes. "At least I have Ivan."

Ivan.... Emily sat up a little straighter in the bed, listening. He was barking again. Emily started to yell at him when her ear caught the faint sound of an idling car engine. Suddenly it revved up and gunned down the dirt road. Ivan barked three more times, and Emily finally yelled at him to hush. Honestly, did he have to bark at every car that passed?

"Give me a break, dog," Emily groaned, plumping her pillow and flopping back. "I'm finally in a position where I don't have to listen to J.J.'s rock music blasting me out of my room or listen to Mom and Dad fighting about what to do with him. I don't have to listen to creaking floorboards when people walk across the floor in the apartment above mine, or hear the water running down the pipes every time they turn on a faucet. I have a home of my own now."

But for how long? The uncertainty lingered even though she hadn't heard from Simon Balfour again. Emily tried to convince herself he had been a slick con artist who had discovered she couldn't be conned, so he had given up. And yet what kind of con artist talked about old hymns and...and called her a sparrow?

The metaphor hurt because sparrows were nondescript, pesky birds everyone ignored.

And yet.... Emily had taken time to run by her church, where she rifled through the pages of an old hymnbook Mrs. Jenkins, the church pianist, unearthed for her. Why *would* a slick con artist talk about God as Simon Balfour had and refer to a song about how God watches over individuals as He does an insignificant bird? It had been a rather comforting song, actually, and when Mrs. Jenkins told her she was welcome to the hymnbook since the church used newer ones now, Emily had accepted the offer with thanks.

Ivan didn't bark again, and eventually Emily slid back into sleep.

The next morning was gray and sullen. Emily donned her jeans and an old, oversize t-shirt with an arrow on the front pointing down to her stomach and the word 'BABY' printed above it. Another arrow beside it pointed upward with the word 'MOTHER' printed at its point. Barb had donated the garment after declaring she would never need it again, teasing Emily about what would happen if Emily wore it in public. Emily had laughed and said it was going to be a work shirt, and if Ivan and Samson took offense, she could shove them both outside.

She had finished stripping and sanding all the wood in the library and was going to start painting a lovely creamy gold color. It would be nice to wallpaper, of course, but that would have to wait. One day....

A light rain started when she had been painting an hour, and with a sigh Emily put the brush down to close all the windows but the two opening to the side veranda. Even if the shower turned into a downpour, the overhanging porch would keep the water from splashing inside and ruining all her work.

Sure enough, within the next hour the sky darkened and rumbles of thunder heralded a good, old-fashioned summer storm. Emily ignored the sound and fury and continued to paint in long, even strokes just like the instructions recommended. It was actually sort of soothing, and she began humming a tuneless song to the rhythm of the strokes, oblivious to the rest of the world. She was so oblivious that she didn't hear Ivan's welcoming barks over the steady beating of the rain on the roof, nor the sound of the buzzer-style doorbell that didn't work half the time anyway.

Balanced on the top step of her new ladder, reaching to paint over the crown molding that framed the walls next to the ceiling, Emily didn't hear the footsteps scraping across the floor and pausing momentarily at the entrance of the library. When Simon Balfour's voice offered in approving tones, "This is looking good," Emily was so startled she let out a small yelp, jerked around, and promptly lost her balance.

She would never know how he managed to move so quickly, but Simon caught her as she toppled, the wildly waving paintbrush missing his head by inches. His arms folded around her in a hard, bruising grip, and for just a moment he held her tightly against his chest before setting her gently on her feet.

"I'm sorry. I suppose I should have kept ringing the bell, but I was getting soaked out there and, besides, I was concerned about you." He stopped, his gaze dropping to the paint-spattered t-shirt, then lifting to search her face.

Emily was still too busy recovering her breath as well as her balance. She lifted her hand to swipe at her hair, saw that she was still clutching the brush, and laid it carefully down across the top of the can of paint. What on earth was he doing here? She straightened slowly, using the brief seconds to marshall her scattered senses. Her eyes lifted to meet Simon's, where the blankness of a stone wall had replaced the engaging air of apology and concern and interest.

That threw her all over again, and instead of demanding to know what he was doing she gaped at him, not understanding the aura of disapproval, almost censure, that hovered behind the carefully expressionless face.

"I wasn't aware of your condition," Simon said finally after a moment of uneasy silence. "It's none of my business, but I don't think it's such a good idea to be perched up on ladders, much less inhaling all these fumes without adequate ventilation."

"Just what," Emily demanded incredulously, "are you talking about? I'm healthy as a Berkshire hog at the county fair, and you're right, it *is* none of your business. Speaking of that, what are you doing here, anyway?"

He was staring at her front again, so fixedly that Emily finally followed suit to see what was causing him to be so abominably rude. Color climbed hectically all over her cheeks; she groaned and covered her face with her hands.

"I will never tell my best friend Barb about this," she mumbled from behind her splayed fingers. "This is one of her old maternity tops she gave me to work in. I'm not pregnant. In fact, I've never—" she stopped, so embarrassed she wanted to leap through the open window and see if the rain would melt her...or maybe lightning would strike her dead....

Simon was laughing. "I'm relieved you're not pregnant," he finally managed to say between chuckles. "I'm also just as pleased to hear about the other, even if that's none of my business, either. Young women like you are a rare and wonderful species nowadays, and speaking as a Christian, and a man, I'd like to ask you to marry me."

Emily jerked back, then realized he was teasing her. It was a kind thing for him to do, and it worked. She found herself laughing, the awkwardness and humiliation of the moment dissolving. "If I wasn't so sure you were asking mainly in order to get your hands on my house, I just might consider accepting and teaching you a lesson," she tossed back.

Simon shook his head and proceeded to wander around the library examining her work. Emily found herself feeling like one of her eighth graders taking mid-terms. Would he truly approve of what she had done? More to the point—

why did she care *what* Simon Balfour thought? Because she was so uncomfortable with the direction of her thoughts, she sidelined the whole issue. "I need to go check on my cat," she blurted. "He's not too wild about thunderstorms."

With cool dignity she marched from the room as if her hair were bound in a strikingly elegant coronet and she were dressed in a suit, silk stockings, and three inch heels.

When she hadn't reappeared in ten minutes, Simon went searching, taking note of the fact that she had moved all her furniture in. The bulk of it was crammed in haphazard fashion in a room down the front hall: boxes stacked on top of each other and tables on top of tables, chairs with their legs stuck up in the air mingling with lamps and knick-knacks and other odds-and-ends. Simon shook his head again, smiling a little at this evidence of Emily Carson's determination to stake her claim. *Hey, Lord, this is a lot harder than I thought it would be*. Why couldn't she be some hard-nosed female who could just be bought off with appropriate monetary compensation? Why a vulnerable, appealing young woman with gumption and grit and the most expressive pair of brown eyes he'd ever encountered?

"I'm storing it in here," Emily informed him from over his right shoulder.

He turned, taking note of the cat purring contentedly in her cradled arms. Not another furry animal to contend with? How many did she have, anyway? She had mentioned the two last week, but Simon was rapidly coming to realize that Emily Carson was an unpredictable creature at best. She just might produce a rabbit or two from under the staircase if he wasn't careful.

"I can see that. What are your plans—a room at a time?

The cat was kneading its paws with the pin-like claws

against her breast. Emily transferred him to her shoulder, where he draped about her neck as contented and limp as only felines can be. "Yes, Emily agreed almost defiantly. "One room at a time, and you saw for yourself how capable I am."

"How would you like a job working for me then? I could always use capable, dedicated help." He watched her closely, wondering how someone with so expressive a face could be so wary and cynical about people.

"If that's a subtle way of re-introducing our previous discussion on a supposed title discrepancy, it worked." She gently dumped the cat on top of what was presumably a cushioned kitchen chair, residing at the moment on top of a coffee table. "Would you like a Coke or something to drink? And come find a chair somewhere. If we're going to fight, we might as well be comfortable."

"A Coke would be nice, and I didn't come wanting to fight you." He followed her into a small galley kitchen with ancient, grease-filmed gas appliances. A small dinette table with metal legs had been positioned under a window, with one of the mates to the chair Emily had put the cat on next to it. Simon backtracked the few steps to the dining room and helped himself to the chair next to the cat, who stared at him with unblinking disdain.

When he returned, Emily handed him a paper cup filled with ice cubes and cola. "I haven't unpacked dishes yet," she said, sounding defensive.

Simon shrugged amiably. "This is fine." He took a long swallow, put the cup down, and leaned forward on his elbows. "Emily, I flew up to Connecticut to try and persuade Aunt Iris to drop the whole thing. She's never even seen this place and has apparently looked on it as sort of a nest egg security for her old age all these years."

"Connecticut?" Emily spluttered. "Why on earth should someone from Connecticut be interested in a house in the backwoods of south Georgia?" She searched his face. "Can you prove any of this today?"

"Yes. I brought papers and letters and identification—I left them in the car, though." He stood, glancing out the window at the pouring rain. "Do I have to go get them right now?"

"No," Emily allowed, relenting in the face of Simon's plaintive plea. "You can wait until it lets up some. But I do want to see some proof of all this."

"I understand. In the meantime, can I explain the situation and try to convince you that I'm as frustrated by it all as you are?"

"I can imagine your level of frustration," Emily responded dryly. "How much profit would you realize restoring a place like this?"

"That," stated Simon a little too evenly, "was uncalled for." Emily ducked her head, but Simon knew she sensed the temper flicking beneath the words.

"I'm sorry." She traced the faint brown stain made from a too-hot pan, her gaze wandering around the room and settling on the stain again. "This was my fault," she murmured absently, as if Simon had asked. "I was twelve. Mom yelled at me about how clumsy and stupid I was. Then—like she always did—she turned around five minutes later and apologized. Another five minutes later she breezed out the door to go—I've forgotten where she went...."

Her voice remained offhand, neutral, but Simon suddenly had the uncomfortable urge to wrap her in a tender embrace. He also had a feeling the scar on Emily's soul was as permanent as the scar on the table.

"Hey."

She lifted her eyes.

"We'll work it out, okay?" Briefly, deftly, he brushed the back of her hand. "I understand the sense of panic and desperation you must be feeling, and I really would like to avoid your losing your home. But unfortunately for us both, there's still Aunt Iris."

"Blood is thicker than water," Emily murmured, but there was no sarcasm in the observation, and she managed to give Simon enough of a smile to convince him she was merely trying to inject a lighter note.

"I don't think Aunt Iris has blood—not her own, anyway," Simon returned. The ensuing laughter was strained, but somehow after that the atmosphere lightened, and when Emily offered to make sandwiches to go with the drinks, Simon agreed easily.

"From what I can gather, my grandmother couldn't have cared less about this property—but then she married my grandfather pretty young and had no need of it anyway." He took another huge bite of his ham and cheese sandwich. "Iris never married, though, and from what Mother tells me she's always had a 'thing' about the 'family estate.' I suppose, when you grow up in the Depression years, land is about as valuable as money in your pocket. Aunt Iris felt that as long as she had the property down in Georgia, she would never have to be beholden to anyone or be totally destitute."

"Where did this"—Emily waved her sandwich—"family estate come from? Who built it? And why here in Georgia instead of Connecticut?"

Simon smiled across at her. The bruised look was fading from her eyes now, and she was almost as relaxed as her cat, who at the moment was sitting at his feet with a hopeful, expectant look on his face. Simon ignored him.

"I'm still working on that one. All my great-aunt can remember is her mother talking about a family scandal and amazement that she would even *consider* having anything to do with this property. I gather it was more or less a taboo subject for my grandmother and Aunt Iris, so little was said until their mother—my great-great grandmother—had died. Some mention of the will and the property were made in her will, and Aunt Iris must have jumped on it like a spinster would an eligible male."

"Watch it, fella. I'm a spinster schoolteacher and take exception to such remarks. Who needs men?"

"Such belligerence," Simon lifted his hands in mock surrender, relieved that she had recovered enough to tease like she had when they first met. "Does this mean I can't make you swoon with a display of all my muscles or my just-as-healthy bank account?"

Emily wrinkled her nose. "Yucch. You would doubtless impress the girls in my science classes, but it doesn't do much for me."

Simon gave in and dropped the last bite of his sandwich to the floor. It disappeared immediately. "I take it you disagree with the biblical observation that it is not good for man to be alone."

His gaze wandered over her smooth, high forehead, the huge brown eyes framed with dark lashes and several spatters of cream-colored paint, traced the line of her cheek and jaw back to her mouth, which at the moment was pressed in a tight line.

She was not used to such a frank, masculine survey. Simon found himself wondering why. She was not particularly beautiful, but there was nonetheless something incredibly appealing about her. "What put you off the male of the species?" he asked.

Emily pondered his question a moment, brow wrinkled in thought. "I never really thought about it like that," she confessed at last. "And it's not that I don't *like* men—I suppose I've just been occupied with other things."

She contemplated her supple, slender fingers. "I've had a job of some kind ever since I was fifteen. There was never any time to date much or do all the other things the kids were doing." She began twirling the end of her braid round and round her fingers. "Besides, I have a younger brother who was pretty wild. I spent a lot of time trying to keep him—and his friends—out of trouble."

Emily flung the braid over her shoulder and stood up, dumping the trash in a paper grocery sack on the floor. "My parents had no idea what to do about J.J., and they quit trying. I finally persuaded him to join the Air Force and he's in Germany now."

She turned back to Simon. "That's enough biography. What about the title dispute? What are you going to do now that your great-aunt refuses to give up her notion of a lost will?"

Simon stood up, too, dumped his trash in the bag, and came to stand in front of Emily. "I'm going to have to try and find the will," he admitted, inwardly wincing at Emily's expression. "She claims it's hidden somewhere in this house. I'd like your permission to search for it."

three

Emily closed her eyes. She should have known what he was going to say, but she was so thrown by the whole situation her brain wasn't functioning. "I don't want you nosing around," she whispered, opening her eyes but avoiding looking at Simon. "And if I let you, and you find the will, it's like I'm signing my own death warrant."

"I know."

She hated it when he spoke like that. Why couldn't he be mean and obnoxious, a bully and a crass gold digger she could fight, someone who was easy to harden her heart against?

"But I also know I have to make the effort," Simon continued, his voice flat, expressionless. "And if I can't do it with your cooperation, I'll have to do my job without it."

Emily changed her mind. It was *very* easy to harden her heart against him. "Go ahead, then. But don't expect any help from me." She scooped Samson off the floor and stalked out the door down the long, narrow hall.

Moments later, Emily heard Simon come into the library. "Go away," she said without pausing in her strokes, her voice husky. "Go look for your stupid will."

"Can I help paint a while instead? The way you're going about it, you're going to smack the brush through the wall any minute." Emily paused in mid-stroke, stared at the section of wall she had been painting, and winced. The strokes of her brush were short and abrupt, almost vicious, and as a consequence the wall was a mess. She laid the brush down, wiped her hands on a rag, and rubbed them over her eyes and face.

"I don't want your help," she muttered tiredly. "Could you please either look for the will or leave? I don't mean to be rude, but I'm not very good company right now." Her gaze bounced off his, then returned to a dejected contemplation of the floor. "I don't know why I'm apologizing. It's your fault I'm in this predicament."

Simon studied her with assessing eyes Emily was afraid saw a lot more than she was comfortable with. His next words confirmed it. "Someday I'd like to find out why you have so little faith in yourself and in other people. I'd like to change that, starting with teaching you to have faith in me and my intentions."

He leaned and picked up the paintbrush and placed it in Emily's hand, closing her limp fingers around the handle. "So I'm leaving you right now, giving you some space. I'll come back to start hunting for the will after you've had a little time to adjust. Try not to let your burdens get you down too much, sparrow-girl."

He left, but it was a long time before Emily could concentrate on painting the library wall. She tried to undo the damage she'd inflicted, but her heart wasn't in it. Grumbling, muttering vague threats, she ended up rummaging around upstairs, looking for Simon Balfour's blasted will.

How, she asked herself furiously as she sneezed and coughed through the dust and dim corners of the upstairs rooms, was she supposed to concentrate on restoring her house when she couldn't even be sure it *was* her house? If she found the stupid document before Simon did she would burn it.

No.... She wouldn't, couldn't do that, even if she could get away with it. She might not be the best Christian on the face of this earth, but she did know right from wrong. Even back in high school, before she committed her life to Christ, she had been unable to cheat on tests, or lie about her whereabouts, or experiment with drugs and sex. It had been such a relief to find out the reason why, thanks to a compassionate, caring college roommate. Her body was the temple of God, and He had laid out specific rules as to its care.

Somehow, though, in the last couple of years, the Lord hadn't seemed to figure as prominently in her life. She had been so busy working, so worried trying to keep J.J. out of trouble, and the last couple of months so...disillusioned with life and people that her faith had more or less taken a back seat.

Wiping her hands on her paint-splattered jeans, Emily trudged down the narrow hall into her bedroom. Over in the corner was the box holding all her important documents and papers. Emily rummaged until she came up with the folder holding all the papers on the house, tugged it out, and began reading.

For almost thirty minutes she sifted through legal jargon and page after page of photostated documents and certifications and contracts. Everything looked straightforward, as it should be: On July 10, she and Mildred Davis, realtor, with a lawyer and secretary as witnesses, had signed all the papers for the property known as the deCourier estate over to Emily Elizabeth Carson.

Mildred's mother had handled the property for the past twenty years or so, but since she had been out of the country, the lawyer hadn't seen any problem with Mildred handling things. No one stepped forward protesting the change in ownership—and as Simon pointed out, virtually the whole town knew what was happening in the office of Shady Tree Realtors.

The only other names Mildred and Emily had been able to unearth in the dusty tomb of the records office at the county courthouse had been someone named VanCleef and some man whose first name was Harold (the last name had smeared to an indecipherable blot). The only other owner had been a woman named Gwinette deCourier.

Emily squinted at all the faded type. Where on earth did Simon's Great-Aunt Iris come into all this? What would happen when all the citizens of Timmons heard—as they would, Emily knew. Human emotions were fickle at best. Emily mentally vowed to gird her armor more tightly against whatever weapons Simon Balfour chose to fire at her.

A week passed. Emily worked with single-minded desperation, falling exhausted into bed at night. Her sleep remained restless, uneasy, and twice more Ivan woke her barking at passing cars. A random thought flitted through her mind that there was a lot more traffic out here in the country than she would have anticipated.

Simon returned late one afternoon, just after the whip-poor-wills began their haunting calls to each other from the woods surrounding the house. Ivan barked and galloped across to meet him. Simon irritably ordered him to get down and go away, wondering again why anyone would want a dog the size and disposition of a bouncing kangaroo.

Emily met him at the door, looking even more like a ragpicker's child. "I wondered when you'd come back," she said, chin up and bristling with defiance.

Simon looked closer, noting the signs of exhaustion and apprehension her tired defiance couldn't hide. "I was going to give you a few more days," he replied, following her inside and into the front hall, "but every night my great-aunt calls both my parents in Florida and me at Timmon's one-and-only motel, to see if I've found anything. And...since you're more or less being dangled on a fraying rope over a precipice, I decided the sooner we resolve things, the better for everyone."

"That was a lovely line," Emily murmured, looking both stunned—and close to tears. "You really sounded as if you meant it." She lifted a hand to mop at the perspiration trickling down her temple, and Simon noticed her trembling fingers. He frowned down at her, then peered over her shoulder into the library. "How long have you been working without a break?" he asked quietly.

Emily shrugged. "Since Barb left this afternoon. She and her two kids brought cookies and lemonade. I don't know. What time is it, anyway?"

"It's going on eight o'clock. Have you eaten anything?"

"Lemonade and cookies."

His frown deepened to a scowl. "You stubborn little mule. You're going to kill yourself over this place if you don't take better care." If he had an ounce of sense, he'd hunt out the blasted will and get it over with.... "Go clean up and put on some decent clothes. I'll take you into Timmons for a meal and come back in the morning to search for the will."

She stared at him as if he'd lost his mind, and Simon didn't blame her. He couldn't believe himself, either.

"Do I have any say-so in the matter?"

Suddenly they grinned at each other, and the aura of

tension evaporated. "No," Simon promised, eyes warm and twinkling now but his stance faintly foreboding. "If you don't do as I ask, I'll take you as you are. We might be refused service in the first couple of places, but I daresay someone will eventually overlook your extreme grubbiness."

"Thanks a lot. I'll go clean up—it will probably only take fifteen minutes or so. Do you want to wait in the kitchen? I don't have chairs set up anywhere else."

"I'll wait on the front porch. Take your time, but hurry."

Simon sat on the porch steps, elbows on his knees, feeling buffeted by conflicting feelings of depression and guilt, excitement and determination. Never in his life had he found himself in such an untenable situation, and he didn't know what to do.

Bowing his head in prayer, he sent up a heartfelt petition for guidance and direction. Solomon had been granted the wisdom to handle two women who claimed the same child; surely he could come up with an approach to offer Aunt Iris and Emily Carson which would achieve a similar resolution. Unfortunately, with Emily he seemed to be losing his ability to remain neutral. He stood when he heard her footsteps crossing the porch, something very unnerving stirring deep inside as she came to stand quietly in front of him.

"I don't have any dresses unpacked," Emily gestured apologetically to her plain khaki slacks and the oversized turquoise sleeveless knit sweater. "Will this do?"

Simon studied her face, bare of any makeup, the vulnerability and openness of her nature shining out at him like a beacon. She had washed her hair and coiled it in a wet bun on top of her head. Drying wisps were already slipping out and feathering her slender neck and forehead, and they seemed to accent the slenderness of her form.

She was not beautiful—she was not really even pretty—but Simon felt a giant hand squeezing his heart. She was somehow beyond either of those trite descriptions, and all he could think of was that she was the most gallant person he had ever known. Her dark brown eyes were filled with worry and fatigue, but she had lifted her chin and was gazing at him with that tiny spark of defiance flickering away, distinguishable even in the purple shadows of early evening.

She had a rare beauty of spirit, yet such a thick veneer of disillusionment, the spirit was only allowed to shine at brief unguarded moments he was beginning to cherish. What had made her the way she was? And what *was* he going to do if and when he found the will?

four

They ate at a steakhouse in Timmons, and Emily—with a challenging gleam in her eye—ordered the most expensive steak on the menu. She had just laughingly promised Simon she would, too, eat every bite when a medium-sized man with carefully combed hair and an intimidating scowl stopped by their table.

"Excuse me, but you're Emily Carson, aren't you?"

Emily looked up, smiling in surprise and anticipation. "Mr. Radford! How are you?" He was the principal of the junior high school in Timmons, and Emily hoped he was going to tell her about the position she had applied for. It had worried her to be without a job more than she had allowed Barb to know.

Mr. Radford ignored her question. "Miss Carson, I've been trying to get in touch with you for a week. You apparently had your phone disconnected in Sylvan and have yet to have one installed in your new place of residence." He paused and added bitingly, "It's very annoying, as I'm sure you agree."

Emily colored. "I finally had my secretary send you a letter Friday, but since I saw you here I thought I'd go on and let you know." Mr. Radford glanced at Simon, who was sitting without moving, watching Emily. "The teacher who was considering retiring changed her mind. There are thus no available openings at this time. Since you do have excellent references, we're keeping your name on file for mid-season replacements. We'd also be happy to use you as a sub."

He glanced at his watch, then over toward the entrance. "It's a shame you don't have any training in foreign languages. The high school is looking for a Spanish teacher."

"I see," Emily said very faintly. "Thank you for telling me, Mr. Radford."

"I'm sorry, Emily," Simon offered after Mr. Radford left. "That's a tough break."

"Yes. First you and your will. Now this. God must not want me around here." Her chin lifted. "But I'm staying. I'll handle it—I'll find another job." She picked up her water glass and took a swallow, put it down and toyed with the silverware until the prickling tears receded and the hot poker in her chest cooled a little.

"Emily—look at me." Emily lifted dull brown eyes. "Don't shut God out, or convince yourself He's trying to crush you in defeat. It's not true—He cares very much what happens to you."

"His eye is on the sparrow, right? I found a copy of the song—it's a nice song." She stared down at her steak. "Maybe God does watch out for sparrows—I don't know. I do know He obviously has more important things on His mind than watching out for *me*." She lifted her gaze back to Simon. "So please don't try to convince me otherwise."

"No."

He said the word softly, but with unyielding emphasis, and Emily felt a shaft of something hot and alien stirring to life deep inside her. "Exactly what do you mean by that?" she asked carefully.

"I mean you're wrong, dead wrong, and I'm going to convince you of it if it takes the rest of the summer. Or longer. I have a crew of well-trained men and women who can function on their own awhile."

He placed his palms flat on the table and leaned across, trapping Emily within the compelling depths of his determined gaze. "You, on the other hand, have no job, a house that might not be yours, and the insane notion that God has turned His back on you. If anyone ever needed to be convinced that God has His loving eye on you at all times, you do. And since I feel responsible for at least half your problems, I plan to be responsible for the solutions as well."

"I want to go home, please." If he thought for one minute she was naive enough to fall for *that* approach.... Abruptly, she shoved her chair back and stood. "Thanks for the meal, but I'm not hungry after all. Please enjoy yours—I'll get a taxi. See you in court, Mr. Balfour."

Shamefully glad to see signs of temper flickering across his face, Emily swiveled and marched out of the dining room. Her behavior was irrational, rude—totally out of character—and her parting shot ridiculously childish. But right now she just didn't care.

Simon caught up with her outside.

"Come on," he said, his voice short, clipped. Cupping her elbow, he added, "I'll take you home."

Emily jerked free. "I'm not a helpless old woman yet! You can take me home only because it'll be *hours* before I could rouse a taxi." Stalking across to his car, she reached for the handle, then rounded on the hovering man at her heels.

All the suppressed rage and denied fear welled up and burst free. She glared up into his shadowed face, almost shaking with emotion. "I don't need you, or your—your pity! And if you ever compare me to a sparrow again, I'll wallop you. They're disgusting little creatures nobody cares two straws about—and that song is wrong!"

His figure loomed above her, radiating temper and something even more ominous. "Maybe," he growled, "just maybe *now's* the time to do what I've wanted to do since the second time we met."

Suddenly his arms wrapped around Emily and she was held immobilized against a damp chest that smelled equal parts of after shave, sweat, and rib-eye steak. Without warning his mouth covered hers and Emily Carson, placid, easygoing schoolteacher, was kissed more thoroughly, more expertly, than she had been in her entire twenty-six years.

When Simon lifted his head at last, Emily gawked up at him, mouth tingling, ears ringing, and all around them moths and gnats fluttered in the wavering streams of yellow light from the restaurant parking lot.

"Oh," she stammered out at last, "I thought you were a...a gentleman ... a *Christian* gentleman."

Simon stared at her as if he couldn't quite believe what he had heard. His gaze moved from her eyes to her mouth, and a muscle twitched in his jaw.

"Being a Christian doesn't mean I'm a eunuch, woman!" He turned away with an infuriated jerk and braced his palms flat on the hood of his little green Jensen-Healy. Head bowed, breathing heavy, he stayed thus for several moments without speaking.

Emily considered and cast aside a baker's dozen comebacks, but she was bitterly aware that nothing could erase the unbelievable naivete of her comment. Nor could she deny the fact that the kiss had somehow transformed all her anger to a far more frightening emotion.

What had possessed her to behave so? She had been kissed before, had even successfully repulsed the heated advances of one of J.J.'s drunken companions. What bewildering alchemy had Simon performed to metamorphose a plain, unexciting woman of humdrum lifestyle into a starry-eyed, pliable creature fairly throbbing with—with passion?

She didn't like Simon, she didn't trust Simon, and he was making her feel all sorts of violent emotions she never would have associated with passion and desire: anger, frustration, helplessness, fear. Yet when his mouth had covered hers, all those seething emotions had swirled into something so sweet, so wildly wonderful, so mindlessly bone dissolving that all she could do was gape at him like a bug-eyed frog and utter foolish banalities.

"What are you standing there for? Waiting for an apology—or seconds?" Simon snapped with unforgivable irritation. She had no idea what he must have read on her face, but after pinching the bridge of his nose between thumb and forefinger, he dropped his hand and said, quite gently, "Get in the car, Emily, and I'll take you home."

Emily obeyed without another word, and they spent the next long minutes in thick silence, the only noise coming from the muted roar of the Healy's engine.

Eventually Simon heaved a sigh. "Did I frighten you?" he asked, the words vibrating with an uncomfortable edge, even though he again spoke quietly. Emily wet her lips. "A little," she admitted just as quietly. "But I frightened myself more. I've never behaved that way in my life—I've never *felt* like that in my life." She almost smiled. "I've got a reputation of sorts as being disorganized but level-headed. Haphazard perhaps—but sane, calm, and dependable."

Simon snorted.

"Well, I *have*...I *am*," Emily retorted. She turned her head away and gazed sightlessly out at the dark, deserted countryside. "Ever since you came into my life, nothing has been the same, including *me*. I wish you'd disappear back into the wilds of Connecticut or wherever you came from and leave me alone."

"I've been on a location in Tennessee, and I'd like nothing better than to get back to the order and sanity of my own life. You've messed my life up as well, Emily Carson," he admitted, Then, after another uncomfortable pause, he added, "I haven't treated a woman like that since I was in my unregenerate twenties. If my father were here, he'd likely be tempted to try and mete out the same discipline he did then." He gave a mirthless chuckle. "Especially now that I'm *definitely* old enough to know better."

Emily's curiosity overcame the sinkhole of apathy and depression into which she was sliding. "What on earth did you do—and how did your dad find out?" she couldn't help asking.

"I was seventeen, thought I was God's gift to the female sex, and came on a little too strong for Janie Beth. She told her folks, her dad called mine...and I was grounded for two weeks as well as being sole man on the clean-up crew for my dad's contracting business."

He smiled briefly, ruefully. "And in the evenings I had to paint the fence that surrounded Janie Beth's house. She wouldn't speak to me, but her parents let me hear an earful, as did her twitty thirteen-year-old sister. I remember begging Dad to let me out of at least that part of my punishment, but he just smiled, and I painted."

"What a monster of a father you must have."

She could just make out the swift turn of his head toward her before he returned his eyes to the road.

"Not at all," he refuted evenly. "I wouldn't have respected him like I do if he *hadn't* come down on me that hard. I deserved it." There was a fractional pause, then he added. "He disciplined me in love as a father should, Emily; he didn't punish me to vent his own frustration. Didn't your father do likewise for you?"

"I never needed much disciplining, and he quit trying with Jimmy-Joe after he ran away when Daddy whipped him the last time. He was only ten, but he was gone for two days. After that I think Daddy and Mom both decided to pretty much consign him to whatever retribution he might reap if he was caught." She twisted her purse strap round and round in her hands. "But I know he and Mom cared for us as much as they could, in their own way, so don't go feeling sorry for me."

"It would be easier to feel sorry for a Venus fly trap," Simon grumbled beneath his breath.

The next instant they were both blinded by a car with its headlights on the bright setting, hurtling around a curve and approaching them fast—on their side of the road. Simon flattened his hand on the horn and wrenched the wheel hard to the right.

The other car swerved at the last moment and careered by them with inches to spare. It had not slackened speed at all, and they heard the tires squealing in the distance as it tore around another bend.

"Are you all right?"

Emily released her death grip on her purse and wriggled her fingers to restore the circulation. "I think so," she said shakily. "He must have been drunk."

"Or high as a kite on drugs. I was talking the other day to the proprietor at the motel where I've been staying. Apparently the police think there might be a gang operating somewhere in this county. Whatever happened to plain old moonshine?"

"There's a problem everywhere. Two of my boys were caught behind the bleachers last spring. It makes me furious and sad all at the same time to see lives wasted like that."

"I'm sorry about your job. I have a feeling that's probably what sent you off the deep end back at the restaurant, wasn't it?"

"It didn't help," Emily muttered.

A short while later they turned onto the dirt lane that led to her house.

"Is that *another* car coming?" she asked, squinting to catch what she thought had been the flash of headlights down the road and through the barrier of the trees.

"I don't see any lights." Simon pulled into the front yard and switched off the motor. In the sudden silence the quiet ticking of the cooling engine sounded inordinately loud. There weren't even any cicadas buzzing or crickets chirping.

And Ivan wasn't barking a welcome.

"I wonder where Ivan is?" Emily opened the door and got out without waiting for Simon. She put fingers to her lips and whistled. The shrill sound rent the night, and after a moment she heard the faint barking of her dog. He was across the field, somewhere in the woods the two of them had explored, and Emily pressed her lips together. Some watch dog, but at least he was okay.

"Will you forget that dog for two seconds and listen to

me?" Simon had come up beside her, but Emily hadn't noticed because, in spite of the moon, the darkness out here was as total as the blackest hole in the universe.

She wished she had remembered to leave on her porch light, especially when Simon commented on it. Emily ignored him and began making her way to the front porch, barely discernible in the faint light of a grudging quarter moon.

"Emily.... I want to apologize."

The words floated across the yard and wrapped themselves around her feet, halting her indignant retreat. For the first time since Emily had walked out on him at the restaurant, Simon sounded like—Simon.

She waited, confused and tentative, listening to his steps swishing through the tall grass and weeds. When he was so close she could feel the warmth of his body, he stopped. Every nerve in Emily's body seemed to tingle with the awareness of his presence.

"Emily—" She heard a thread of laughter in the word, "I still disagree with your description of sparrows, but will you at least forgive me for everything else?"

The last of her indignation softened to a bewildering compliance, and Emily heard herself murmur back in just as whispery a tone, "I guess so." Then, her resolve stiffening slightly, she stepped back away from him and added with a hint of vinegar, "Maybe I better find out what you're asking forgiveness for. Your arrogance, your bad temper, or your—your—"

"My what, Emily?"

Oh, no, there it was again. That wretched note of laughter dancing through otherwise ordinary words, playing a pied piper tune on her heartstrings. Confound the man, anyway. What had he done to her? "Your kiss!" she flung out recklessly as she braced herself for his laughter.

It never came. What did come was a very wet, very dirty Ivan leaping out of the night and practically knocking Emily down. He yapped and whined and panted, his forepaws leaving muddy trails all over her clothes, arms, and legs. His bullwhip tail snapped happily against Simon, who kept dodging about trying to avoid the affectionate welcome.

"Oh, Ivan, bad doggie! Where were you? Stop that—why weren't you guarding the house?" She laughed harder when Ivan turned to Simon, who snarled at the dog to leave him alone. Emily ordered Ivan to the porch. "What's the matter?" she intoned innocently. "Don't you like my dog?"

"Not particularly. He's about as lovable as a dead elephant, and he smells like a sewer."

"He smells like a dog," Emily retorted, stung by the acerbic answer. "He can't help that anymore than you can help smelling like a man!" After one horrible second with those last words ringing in her ears, she added in a much smaller voice, "I didn't mean that the way it sounded."

Simon didn't answer. He had turned away, and he was laughing so hard the sound echoed back from the woods and fields. Emily decided his laughter was one part humor and three parts hysteria, with a dollop of resignation and frustration tossed in for effect. She walked slowly over to the porch steps and sat down on the bottom one. Ivan whined, but she told him to stay. Simon was at least partly right: at the moment he did smell a lot like a sewer.

"I give up," She heard Simon eventually gasp out

between chuckles. "I think it's a waste of time trying to accomplish anything with you tonight. We can talk in the morning when I come back to start looking for the will."

The will. In the emotional turmoil of the past hour Emily had virtually forgotten the reason for Simon's presence in the first place.

He must have heard her involuntary gasp. "Try not to worry," he promised in a voice as dark and calm as the night. "And try to find it in your heart to forgive me—for everything—Emily Carson."

"Simon...." It was difficult to squeeze his name past the constricted muscles of her throat.

"Will you go inside before I leave and at least turn on the porch light?" His voice floated back across the yard. "With the dog I feel a little better leaving you, but I'd still like to know you're safe inside."

How could someone who had made her angrier than she had ever been in her life turn around and make her feel more protected, and, well, *cared* for than she had ever been in her life? "All right."

She stood listening until the sound of his car faded away. When Ivan poked his nose in her hand and pressed his wet body against her, she cupped his head and held him close. At this moment his presence, smell and all, was all that stood between her and a vast chasm of loneliness.

five

Two days later Simon returned, driving—to Emily's outraged disbelief—a pickup truck which was towing a pop-up style camper.

A wry smile lifted the corners of his mouth. "If your phone were installed, I would have called to let you know," he said, correctly reading Emily's indignation. Stepping past her, he looked around the empty foyer, into the freshly painted but still bare library, and finally back at Emily.

"It really bothers me, you know, you being out here by yourself with no way to call for help. Which is why, of course—" he gestured toward the camper. "This is my `portable office' that I had one of my guys bring down from Tennessee. I borrowed the truck from the gas station to bring it here so Charlie could take my truck on back to Tennessee."

"You're as bad as my best friend, Barb," Emily groused wearily, at the same time feeling a shameful twitch of relief. "Look, the phone man will be here as soon as he can. Until then, you will all just have to add a few gray hairs to your heads. I've got a few myself after the other night."

"What happened the other night?" The small smile hovering on his lips suddenly widened. "Or are you referring to our cat and dog fight?"

Her cheeks warmed. "I'm referring to the fact that it took me almost forty-five minutes to find Samson, and when I did, he was as strung out as if he'd been tossed between two pit bull dogs, and then I heard—" she skidded to an abrupt halt, not feeling up to facing any more of Simon's bullying concern.

"What did you hear, Emily?" He was looking really concerned now, and Emily grimaced.

"Oh, nothing that out of the ordinary," she tossed out offhandedly. "Just a car that sounded like it was going to stop but changed its mind when Ivan barked."

Simon looked like a lovely white, puffy cloud suddenly burgeoning into a towering thunderhead, and Emily hastened to add, in an attempt to downplay the incident, "I'm sure they were lost and probably needed directions. If they had known Ivan was more of a puppy dog than a watch dog, I'm sure they would have come in and asked for coffee as well as directions."

"It's a good thing I decided to camp out here until I find the will."

He was glowering at her as if Emily were a naughty, rebellious child, and instantly her defenses sprang up. "I haven't granted you permission to move in," she hissed, wanting to gnash her teeth, wanting to kick his shins. "Just because I'm a woman doesn't mean I don't know how to take care of myself. Why do men always have to think like that?"

Good grief! What's the matter with me? Slapping her palms over her flushed cheeks, Emily averted her head and moaned, "Look what you do to me! Simon, I can't *do* this. I'm not constitutionally set up for these kinds of games."

"Neither am I," Simon drawled, looking faintly dangerous. "Let's kiss and make up and start all over." He reached out a lazy arm and folded her into his embrace. "I need to amend your way of thinking about men. *Christian* men, anyway."

"There's nothing wrong with the way I think about men, Christian or otherwise," Emily shoved his chest. He was wearing a creamy yellow, button-down chambray shirt and shorts instead of jeans. He smelled of soap and something minty, and with his green eyes boring into her from close range she realized a few other things about men she hadn't known before. She hadn't realized she could feel this way about one. "Simon, why are you behaving like this?"

His eyes softened, and he dropped a quick, undemanding kiss on her wrinkled forehead and released her. "I don't know," he answered with disarming honesty. "I find you very attractive, but you also frustrate and infuriate me more than any woman I've ever known. And with the situation over the house and Aunt Iris swinging back and forth between us like Edgar Allan Poe's pendulum, my behavior comes across accordingly."

Emily pondered him, nose wrinkled along with her brow as she mulled over the implications behind his words. Men had dated her infrequently over the past years, but usually it was because she was always available, or a good shoulder to cry on about their real girlfriends or because Emily needed an escort and asked for the date herself. No one had ever mentioned the fact that she was attractive.

She shook her head, and the freshly wound braid swung back and forth along her slumping shoulders. "Let's go find the will," she stated tiredly. "That's about all I can think of right now."

She started up the stairs without a backward glance, but when she reached the top she paused, turning back to Simon. "The next time you grab me and kiss me, you'd better be prepared to nurse a sore jaw."

A dangerous spark glinted in the depths of his enigmatic green eyes. "We'll see," he murmured, and they proceeded in silence to the room at the head of the stairs.

Three hours and three inches of dust and grime later, Emily called a halt. "We've searched every inch and it's not up here. It probably doesn't exist, anyway. Why can't your aunt accept that?"

"You haven't met my aunt." Simon considered the weary, bedraggled young woman in front of him. "Would you give up this house without a fight?"

Emily sighed and admitted painfully, "No. What are we going to do?"

Simon sank down onto the floorboards and leaned back against a wall. His grimy hands worried his matted, damp hair, causing the waves to curl even more wildly about his face and ears. Tracings of dust and perspiration trickled down his face, emphasizing the lines of weariness marring his countenance. He looked up at Emily and sighed. "I'm afraid, Miss Carson, that you're going to have to talk to a lawyer."

Bradley Lauderman's office consisted of two rooms over what used to be Sylvan's only theater. Emily had chosen to go to a lawyer in her home town because she needed the emotional support of familiar surroundings. Barb's husband, Taylor, had recommended Bradley Lauderman, as had her old principal Joe Southers, so Emily was hopeful of sound advice for what she also hoped would be a reasonable price. After her appointment, she planned to run over to the school and throw herself at Joe's mercy, beg him to re-hire her, even as a janitor.

Simon had wanted to accompany her to this appointment. In the last several days, along with searching for the will, he had offered advice on everything from the security of her home to the refinishing of her home to refinishing herself. ("Emily, you can't exist on a diet of cheese crackers and soup—you already bear an uncomfortable resemblance to a starving rock star, especially when your hair looks like that." Emily had thrown the sticky paint rag at him and told him if he was going to criticize the least he could do was shave his head to control his own untidy hair.)

In contrast to his earlier behavior, Simon was now scrupulously treating her like his kid sister. Emily knew he worried about her—and not just concerning her eating habits and casual appearance. The night before her appointment with Bradley Lauderman, Simon had also heard a car idling outside. Peering through the window of his camper, he watched a car door ease open. When Ivan barked inside the house, it immediately slammed shut and the car left.

Subdued, even surly all morning, he and Emily finally had it out over the matter, with Emily ending the discussion abruptly by bursting into tears. Even now she squirmed when she remembered her behavior. Or at least that's what she kept telling herself. But she had a nagging suspicion that her real discomfort was with Simon's response.

Following her out onto the back porch, trapping her against the railing, he took her chin in his hand and just stared at her in silence for a long uncomfortable moment. "You're the most stubborn woman I've ever known," he repeated, only this time his voice crooned the words instead of shouting. "But you're also a rare and precious jewel, Emily Carson, even though you can't see it."

His thumbs brushed away her angry tears, and then she was free. "God help me," he muttered fervently then, "because I *can* see it, and that's why you scare me into losing my temper with you." Emily could only stare dumbly.

Simon turned away, so she was not totally certain of his last sentence. "And if someone tries to harm you in any way, God help me for what I would do to them," was what she thought he had said.

That sounded much too romantic and dramatic a statement for a man to make about a woman like her, so Emily tried to shrug the whole incident aside and focus her distracted senses on the encounter with Bradley Lauderman.

Shrugging Simon aside, however, was about like trying to shrug off the Rock of Gibraltar.

Climbing the narrow steps to Bradley Lauderman's office, Emily found that her stomach muscles were clenching and her hands were damp. She opened the dusty, glass-topped door reluctantly, and from the other side of a cluttered desk, a young smiling woman with dark curly hair greeted her.

"Hi. Emily Carson?"

Emily nodded, absorbing the old, sagging chairs, the framed prints of different species of duck hanging crookedly on the walls. Old magazines were scattered on the low table in front of the chairs. Her gaze swung back to the secretary, who had risen from behind the desk. She smiled into Emily's widening eyes.

"I'm due any day and look like a watermelon, I know. But Brad desperately needs the help so I'm hanging in there."

From behind a closed door a man's voice called, "Is that

Ms. Carson, Gloria?" The door opened and a tall slender man stepped through. He had a glorious thatch of straw-colored hair and blue eyes that crinkled at the corners. In spite of the fact that it was late summer, his skin was untanned, but he radiated energy and vitality. He held out his arm and shook hands with Emily. "Come on in. We don't stand on ceremony around here. Gloria, can you waddle across the hall and wheedle some coffee from Dave?"

"For you, anything."

As the secretary disappeared, Brad grinned down at Emily. "Dave's a CPA—has an office across the hall. He's so agreeable about sharing his coffeepot, we never got around to installing one of our own." As he ushered Emily into his private sanctum, he winked. "It also cuts down on the exorbitant rates I have to charge my clients."

Emily was charmed by his easy wit and manners. Some of her anxiety began to dissipate, and as she relaxed back into an old but comfortable wingback leather chair she looked around. Brad Lauderman's office was a mess. All four walls were covered floor to ceiling with legal books, documents, and papers. They even surrounded the three metal filing cabinets, one of which had a drawer left open, a file tilted upward at an angle. Emily felt uncomfortably at home.

"Don't look so worried. All lawyer's offices look like this."

She met his teasing eyes with a grin. "Actually, it reminds me of my own place. Organized chaos."

"Exactly." He reached across his desk to a glass jar filled with all shapes and sizes of gum, from sticks to colored balls to Bazooka bubble and huge grape spheres. He caught

Emily's rapt interest. "I gave up smoking and got hooked even worse on this." He gestured to the jar and popped one of the smaller balls. Then he leaned back in his desk chair, clasping his hands behind his head and keeping his intent gaze upon Emily. "Now, what's the problem? I've been over all the stuff you had Roger Bates send me. Tell me everything. I don't have to be at court until noon."

Emily took a deep breath. "I better start off by method of payment. If I can't have my old teaching position back, I'll be an unemployed schoolteacher, with the reason I'm here a heavy albatross about my neck."

"That could be a problem, I agree." He sat forward, glancing down at some papers on his desk before looking at Emily again. "Can you type?"

"Yes," Emily answered, though her voice was bewildered.

"Great!" Brad rubbed his palms together, a wide grin splitting his face. "Then I think we might have a solution to both our problems."

An hour later Emily was still protesting, but much less vigorously. Bradley Lauderman wanted her to replace Gloria as his secretary for a couple of months.

"...By which time you might have found another teaching position, and hopefully the situation with your house will be resolved." He blew a huge bubble, caught sight of Emily's poorly hidden amusement, and sheepishly grinned. "Sorry. I forget sometimes how unprofessional that must look." He swallowed the bubble. "I have warned you, though, that this could drag on for up to six months, depending on a number of factors."

"I know." Emily contemplated her neat but worn taupe pumps a minute, then looked back across the desk in confused indecision. "I still feel uncomfortable with the whole idea of a lawsuit, not to mention working for you while you're more or less working for me."

Brad smiled back in sympathy. "It might raise a few brows about conflict of interest, but we're in Sylvan, not Chicago, and the whole town has known both of us since we were in diapers." He swept a non-professional, frankly masculine survey over her person. "How is it that you and I have missed each other all these years?"

"I was probably still in pigtails chasing after my brother and his friends, making a pest of myself, and you were probably chasing after all the girls in high school making a pest of yourself."

"Hey—I'm not that many years your senior!" He picked up the notes he had taken in the past hour and studied them a few minutes. "If you've given me all the facts, there's a mere six years separating us. Want to complicate our relationship even further by having dinner with me tonight?"

"No," Emily shook her head in mock dismay. "I'm confused enough by this whole mess as it is and besides, I just wouldn't feel...comfortable. Mr. Lauderman... Brad...do you really have to file a lawsuit?"

He instantly reverted to the seasoned professional lawyer. "Yes, Emily, that is the correct legal procedure. As far as I'm concerned you aren't violating any biblical tenets about suing your brother, or whatever the phrasing is. You are merely following legal precedent for the express purpose of determining who has superior title to the property." He stood up, stretching his tall, lanky frame. "Trust me as your lawyer, all right? If you have any more questions about the religious end of it, why don't you talk to Sam Noland? Isn't he the minister of the church you attend?"

Emily nodded and stood up as well. "I don't feel comfortable about working for you either, even if you are deducting your fee out of the paycheck." She paused, then leveled a straight look at him. "You still won't be charging me what you normally would, will you?"

"Nope, but at least I'll have a secretary, and that matters a heck of a lot more to me than losing a few bucks." He came around the desk and held out his hand. "Let's shake on it, Ms. Emily Carson."

"But I haven't typed in years, and although I was a secretary for Mr. Evans when he was mayor, I was all of seventeen years old. I've probably forgotten—"

A stick of peppermint gum was thrust into Emily's mouth, and her hand was grasped in a warm, firm handshake. "Chew on that instead of problems that don't exist," Brad admonished her easily. He held her hand a little longer than was strictly necessary, but immediately let go when she tugged. "Set up a time to get together with Gloria and she can show you the ropes. Don't wait too long, though, or you might be winging it as you go."

His intercom buzzed, and he stretched a long arm to take the call. He held his hand over the mouthpiece and finished by saying, "Gloria will set up our next 'business' appointment—or you can do it yourself if she's gone into labor or something."

Emily left the office shaking her head in bemusement, and another hour later she left the building still shaking her head. Gloria had been so relieved she had thrown her arms about Emily and hugged her, then laughed at the awkwardness of her gigantic stomach. She had also asked if Emily had time to learn the ropes now, since she might not, as Brad pointed out, have another opportunity.

The job seemed simple enough. She would basically be fielding phone calls, typing up wills, filing, and a couple of times a week walking the two blocks to the courthouse to file a client's papers with the clerk of the court when Brad was unable to do it. Because she was still trying to restore the house herself, and because he wasn't that overloaded with cases, she would only be working three days a week, leaving her plenty of time to work on her home.

"Since the paperwork from the lawyer who handled the closing on your property indicates that you have good title to the property, keep on with the sanding and painting if that's what cranks your engine," Brad had reassured her.

six

Emily decided to detour by Barb's house instead of going straight home. She hadn't seen her friend or been able to talk to her in a week, and although she might fuss and worry, Barb was a marvelous sounding board. She also had rock-bed common sense, easing Emily's mind over Simon's ubiquitous presence in her life. Taylor, in fact, verbalized their relief that Emily wouldn't be isolated anymore.

Today, however, when Barb opened the door she gave a relieved shriek, grabbed Emily's arm, and hauled her into the house. "Mark, turn down the stereo!" she yelled, and as they passed the table in the entrance hall, she swiped up a newspaper. "Look at this." She thrust the paper under Emily's nose. "Look at it! I've been out of my mind worrying."

Emily read the headlines, mouth dry. "Car Overturns on County Road—Kills Two Passengers." The subtitle noted that a second wrecked car had been found abandoned near the site of the accident, with several pounds of cocaine and two boxes full of pornography found in the trunk. Identities were being withheld on the dead passengers until more details were known.

The road was the road that led to Emily's house. The time of the accident placed it on the night she and Simon had almost been run off the road.

"That doesn't mean it was right outside my front door, Barb," she began somewhat weakly.

Barb, who had poured herself a glass of iced tea and grabbed a couple doughnuts while Emily was reading, promptly slammed down the glass. "Front door, my Great-Gramma's nightshirt! When are you going to come to your senses, Em? The world is not a safe place anymore, especially for someone like you."

"I can take care of myself."

"That's just the problem," Barb argued, sighing and gulping the tea and doughnuts as she tried to make her point. "You've always had to take care of yourself, and you have no idea how really vulnerable you are. Simon won't be around forever, you know. Someday, something is going to happen and you're going to realize you need other people, and they won't be there—especially when you've isolated yourself out in the boonies."

Emily drove home through a late afternoon thundershower, moody and depressed. Not only was she unnerved by the newspaper article and Barb's consequent flapping, but even more by her friend's observation on her own self-reliance.

Emily had always prided herself on her independence, her ability and determination to do anything she set her mind to, even if she had the knack for biting off more than she could chew. She hadn't really had much choice. It didn't do to try and depend on other people—they only let you down eventually, as she had learned throughout her lonely life. It was simply short-sighted to depend too heavily on other people when the only person you could really count on was yourself.

Sure, God figured in it all somehow, Emily supposed. And maybe in some remote sense He cared about her.

But she couldn't worry Him with all her problems when the world had so many worse ones, could she? Wars, famines, disease—the Lord depended on *her* to keep the oils of her own unremarkable life running smoothly, freeing Him for all the big-time stuff.

It was far better to be kind and friendly to everyone, live by the Golden Rule, but never expect or hope for anything in return. That way, she would not be disappointed and let down when something happened like Simon Balfour appearing out of the blue and threatening to take her house away from her.

A long rumble of thunder pealed across the rain soaked countryside, and a thin streak of lightning zigzagged across the sky. *He makes me feel about like this storm*, Emily reflected as she slowed down to allow for the torrential onslaught. Telling her God has His loving eye on her all the time, promising he would help find solutions to her problems. Ha! Simon *was* the problem, with his grass green eyes and his silver tongue...calling her a sparrow and...and kissing her like...like he couldn't help himself any more than Emily could control her own response.

I won't be an easy mark. I may be easygoing—but I'm not an easy mark. She turned onto the dirt lane which, because of the rain, was a sea of mud, and wriggled her tense shoulders. She wouldn't be an easy mark as long as Simon kept his hands to himself.

It was an infuriating admission, but she might as well be honest with herself. She was attracted to the man, regardless of all the circumstances muddying her life as the rain muddied the road. She was almost glad he hadn't found the will yet, not because it meant she would keep her house, but because it kept him near.

Okay...she was a borderline easy mark and would just have to try harder.

Pulling into the yard, Emily sternly ordered her heart to be relieved instead of depressed that Simon's car was gone. Ignoring the lack of an umbrella, she slogged up the porch steps, drenched and dreary—and gasped in alarm. Ivan sprawled limply in the corner, not even a flicker of movement from his tail greeting her. He had been sick, and specks of foam lined the corners of his mouth. She rushed to his side, heart hammering. "Ivan, what happened? What's wrong?"

A vet. She needed to call a vet. She was scrabbling frantically in her purse for the key when the brutal fact hit home: She had no phone.

"Ivan," she sobbed beneath her breath. "Lord, please don't let anything happen to Ivan."

Another crack of thunder and a simultaneous lightning flash heralded a fresh downpour. Paying no attention to a note taped to the door, Emily unlocked the house, ran to her bedroom, and yanked off the spread. Halfway down the hall she stopped, remembering how Samson hated storms.

She dropped the spread, ran back into the dining room, and found the cat in his hiding place behind the boxes. Scooping him out, she took him to the kitchen and poured him some milk, spilling half of it all over the counter in her haste. After reassuring him that the storm would pass and begging him to forgive her for leaving him, she dashed back down the hall, grabbing the spread as she ran.

Two hours later Emily drove home alone, having left

Ivan overnight at the vet's for observation. Her hands shook when she at last unlocked the door and untaped Simon's note. He'd had to run off to Tennessee again and would be back the next afternoon. He was sorry to leave her alone again.

Alone. Emily wadded the paper into a ball and called for Samson in a voice that did not sound at all like her own. When the cat wandered out to the hall and stropped himself against her legs as if he hadn't a care in the world, Emily finally broke down.

It did not occur to her that *she* might be in danger.

The next afternoon she was getting ready to retrieve Ivan when Simon drove up.

"What's wrong?" he asked immediately, looking solid and secure and scruffy in faded cut-offs and a paint-stained t-shirt from Alaska advising "Go kiss a moose."

Under any other circumstances she would have teased him about trying to emulate her own dress style. Unfortunately, not even rags dimmed the intensity of his discerning gaze or the attractiveness of his smile, which was fading fast in light of her awkward silence. "I have to go to town," she answered, nose buried in her purse. "You can come on in and start searching if you want to. I...I'll be back in awhile."

Firm fingers lifted her chin. "I asked what's wrong," Simon repeated gently. "You've been crying."

Startled, Emily pulled free, her hands clutching confusedly at her shoulder bag. "How can you tell?" she asked.

Simon stuffed his hands in the waistband of his shorts and contemplated her a moment. "Your eyes are slightly puffy and your nose is still red." His voice suddenly changed, became abrupt, almost cold. "Are you going back to the lawyer? Is what he told you yesterday so upsetting it made you cry?"

"No...Brad was very nice. In fact, I'm going to be his—" she stopped, unwilling to go into the details when all she could think about right now was Ivan. She started to brush past Simon. "I'll tell you about it later. I really need to go right now."

"You're going to be his what?"

Hard hands with a grip that was not gentle at all latched onto her shoulders and jerked her around. He held her at arms' length, and the look on his face was indescribable. "Emily, what have you done?" When she looked up at him uncomprehendingly he shook her. "What have you done to keep this house, you idiot?" he repeated, his voice so full of fury and panic Emily's shaky composure erupted as well.

"Let *go!* What's the *matter* with you? Brad said it would be all right since it was Sylvan and not Chicago. I'm sorry if you don't like it but it's really none of your business what I do." She squirmed uncomfortably, then gasped as he thrust her from him, whirled away, and banged his fists on the wall.

Indignation fizzling, Emily took one hesitant step and touched his shoulder. It was like touching one of the sun warmed boulders by a river where she used to vacation as a child. "Simon?" she offered tentatively, wondering at the violent emotion she seemed to generate in him. "There was nothing you could do. It's a job, anyway, and will at least pay the bills. I told Brad I hadn't been a secretary since I was seventeen, but he was desperate because Gloria is due to have her baby any day. I'll be—"

Simon turned back around abruptly and his arm shot out to steady her with an almost convulsive grip. "Did you say *secretary?*" he demanded, a beseeching note beneath the question.

Emily tugged ineffectively at his hand. "Yes." Her own voice reflected her growing bewilderment. "Didn't I tell you?"

Simon released her, lifted a hand to his brow, and closed his eyes. "No," he murmured very quietly, "you forgot to mention that little fact."

"I'm sorry," Emily sighed distractedly. "It's just that I'm so upset about Ivan I don't really know whether I'm coming or going." She paused, gulped, and added, "Speaking of which, I do have to go. Dr. Moffat promised Ivan would be all right, but I won't believe it until he's back here...."

Her voice started to crack and she bit her lip hard. Oh, no. She couldn't break down in front of Simon again. Besides, he didn't like Ivan. He wouldn't understand.

"Ivan? Your dog?" He stepped closer, and Emily tried to smile.

"Someone tried to poison him last night. I got him to the vet in time, but apparently it was touch and go for a while." She swallowed hard. "I'm going to go get him now. Dr. Moffat kept him overnight for observation."

"Ahh..." With heart-stopping tenderness he folded her into an embrace so radically different from his earlier behavior that Emily's defenses collapsed like the walls of Jericho. She clung to him, savoring the heady sensation of leaning on someone else's arms. It wouldn't last but a minute, she knew, but it felt so good. It felt so...nurturing. And she needed it so desperately.

"I'm sorry, honey," Simon was whispering into her hair. "I know how much your dog means to you. What a rotten thing to happen on top of everything else." One hand stoked the long braid, her back, and shoulders, while the other held her close. "That's why you've been crying, isn't it?"

Head buried in the soft t-shirt, Emily could only nod.

Simon continued to hold her, his own thoughts whirling and gradually steadying as he was able to accept that Emily was here, in his arms, and unchanged. There were still a lot of unanswered questions, however, and a lengthy examination of his *own* feelings would have to have top priority over the next few days.

Emily amazingly enough had not picked up on his initial train of thought concerning her relationship with the lawyer. Thank heaven for that, Simon told himself with grim amusement. What a fool he would have looked! He had lost control with her at least twice now, and although she was obviously still totally unaware of the effect she had on him, she was not a stupid woman. She was only confused, worried, staggering beneath problems that would have defeated most other people.

Simon tried to serve his Lord in the best way he could, but it did not always come easy. He had accepted Christ as his Savior when he was fourteen, been a model student through high school and college. Then, after Dad retired from his small construction firm and Simon took over and channelled it into one specializing in restoration, he somehow sidetracked onto the road of hard work and "loose women," as Mother had put it.

One day Mom cornered him, sat him down, and looked him straight in the eye. "Son, do you eventually plan to marry and raise a family like your brother and sister have?" she had asked, casually enough so he hadn't immediately bolted.

"Yeah, one day, Mom. I'm too busy right now, you know. Twenty-seven's not exactly over the hill, and I'd like to have a good time for awhile yet, I suppose...."

"Hmmm," Mom replied. "Well, when you do settle down, do you think it would be with a woman like the ones you've been—seeing—over the last few years?"

Not too much seemed to escape his mother, even if he hadn't lived at home since college. "Good grief, no!" Simon had exclaimed ruefully, but with heartfelt certainty. "Not *those* women...."

She had leaned forward then, planting strong, work-roughened hands on her knees and fixing upon him her most serene, impossible- to-argue-with stare. "So what makes you think a pure Christian woman whom I presume *is* your idea of a suitable mate would have anything to do with a man who dates the type of women you do?'"

He had never forgotten the lightning bolt of conviction that electrified his senses. It had killed his former lifestyle as dead as the bolt that had struck a white pine in their back yard the previous year. Simon had never viewed women in the same manner since, nor treated them as if they were merely there for his personal gratification.

Over Emily's head he smiled. Emily would doubtless disagree. In the weeks they had come to know each other, he had wrecked her carefully constructed little world, bullied her, lost his temper, kissed her with a ruthless passion she had obviously never experienced, and just now had leaped to a regrettable conclusion for which Emily could justifiably take offense. What a mess!

And now that ugly leviathan of a dog had gotten himself poisoned. Who on earth would do such a thing, when Emily lived in such isolated splendor? And why? Some very unpleasant possibilities were nudging his brain, clamoring for attention and causing the muscles of his jaw to clench. Emily had not exactly made a secret of the fact that she lived out here all alone. And those cars—not to mention his talk with the county sheriff about a crash along Emily's road a few weeks back. He wondered if Emily knew about that.

Unfortunately, poisoning the dog might have been more than an arbitrary, haphazard piece of cruelty. Somewhere out there, somebody just might be planning for one Emily Carson to be his next victim.

seven

Surprisingly, Simon went with Emily to pick up Ivan, who was fine, but subdued. Simon spent several minutes talking to Dr. Moffat while Emily paid the bill, made arrangements to bring Samson in to be neutered within the next month, and got Ivan into the car. She couldn't help but wonder why a man who was by and large disinterested in animals would want to talk to a vet. Even after Simon's reply to her query had been an evasive, "Just talking," she was so relieved to have Ivan back, she shrugged the matter aside.

Once they were back at the house and Ivan was ensconced safely in his favorite spot on the front porch, Emily announced that she was going to start painting the kitchen. Simon, as far as she was concerned, was welcome to wear himself out looking for the will wherever he pleased.

"Brad said since the title at present establishes my clear ownership, I can work on the house if I want to," she announced defiantly, expecting a fight.

To her utter astonishment Simon agreed it was probably better that way anyway, but would she promise to break for lunch? He touched the back of his hand to her cheek in a gesture somehow more intimate than a kiss and disappeared upstairs.

For the next two weeks they worked in relative harmony, pursuing their chosen tasks. Their work was interrupted only twice: once by a brief visit from Barb and then by the long-awaited installation of the phone line.

Emily decided Simon must be going over the entire house board by board, and at odd moments when she was particularly tired came to the conclusion he was dragging it out for the sole purpose of annoying her. Several days he prowled outside somewhere, and at other times he worked at a drafting table he'd set up in the library. A couple of times a week he worked outside in the camper in his on-site office, complete with impressive computer, modem, and printer.

Emily had a sneaking suspicion he was also secretly daydreaming about how *he* would restore her house. Her suspicions were confirmed late one Monday afternoon in early September, her third week as Brad's secretary.

It had been a long day, for she was accustomed to standing in front of a blackboard or painting walls, not sitting behind a desk answering the phone, typing, and when she was bored because the phone hadn't rung, updating and reorganizing Brad's files. That day he'd warned her they could expect to hear soon from Iris Bancroft's lawyer, and then the judge could determine the date for their hearing.

As she drove home from work, Emily thought about how she hated the whole process. She felt dreadful knowing she was having to destroy an old woman's dreams, even though Iris was responsible for initiating the whole affair. Of course, from what Simon shared with her, his great-aunt was about as helpless an old woman as Emily was a candidate for Miss America.

Emily hoped the hearing would be soon. Brad was

confident of a verdict in her favor, but that was only because as yet, Simon had not unearthed the will.

As the weeks had passed, Emily had grown more convinced the document didn't even exist, and she suspected Simon agreed, though he wouldn't say so. He never mentioned the hassle he endured whenever he called home (always using his credit card).

Emily had come to know whenever Simon's parents had heard from Iris. He never complained, but there would be a certain tension in the grim line of his mouth, and he would work with fanatical single-mindedness until lunch, when he was finally able to shrug aside whatever wounds the woman inflicted with her incessant goading. Privately Emily was grateful Simon had adamantly forbidden his parents from revealing Emily's new phone number under any circumstances.

He had reverted to the calm, courteous stranger she had first met, neither shouting at her and trying to tell her what to do, nor attempting to approach her romantically. When Emily had realized she felt *slighted* by this decorous behavior, she was so angry with her unruly emotions she erected her own formidable barriers, mostly consisting of a combination of offhand aloofness and determined cheerfulness.

Emily's musings were interrupted as she turned into her driveway. Climbing wearily out of the car, she saw Simon sitting on the front porch steps, incredibly enough tossing a stick for Ivan to fetch. While he had never made overt gestures of friendship to the dog, ever since the poisoning episode he had at least been civil, both to Ivan and Samson. Emily smiled as she walked across the yard to them.

Ivan loped across to her side, barking and posturing

and as healthy as if he hadn't been inches from death less than a month ago. Emily hugged him and talked doggie drivel all the way to the porch, where Simon had risen to meet her.

"Hi." She always felt awkward and shy around him now, never knowing what to say. "Thank you for playing with Ivan. He gets sort of lonely now that I have to be gone three days a week."

"I know," was the dry retort. "He brought the stick over and whined for ten minutes until I finally gave in."

Emily smiled, hating herself for the warm flush she felt rising in her cheeks. "I'm sorry you think he's a nuisance."

"I'm getting used to both of them," Simon promised, stuffing his hands into the hip pockets of a pair of worn out cords.

He followed Emily into the house and down to the kitchen. Gesturing her to a chair, he fixed her a glass of iced tea, then sat down across from her and propped his elbows on the table. "The questions is, are you getting used to *me*, Emily?"

The question was soft but provocative. Emily searched his face, really looking at him for the first time since the day Ivan was poisoned. The green eyes were narrowed, full of light, and very intent on her reaction, but they revealed nothing. His hair was as wild and unruly, just brushing his ears and neck. Right now it looked as if he had just washed it, and the late afternoon sunlight highlighted the gold and chestnut tones Emily so envied. His tan had faded somewhat, and there were lines scoring his cheeks and forehead she hadn't noticed before. "I suppose so," she finally told him slowly. "Why do you ask?" Simon dropped his gaze a minute, contemplating the table as if it contained some secret message. Then the heavy straight lashes lifted, and Emily found herself unable to avoid the piercing intentness of those eyes. "I want to help you restore the house," he told her, the words slow and deliberate so she could not possibly misunderstand. "Not as the professional, not by bringing in my crew and taking over. Just me, helping you, because I've come to...." He hesitated, as if he were still picking his words carefully. "To care about this place almost as much as you have."

Emily, of course, was not surprised. She was, however, staggered by the tidal wave of relief surging over her. Had she somehow let slip these past weeks how uncertain she was of her ability to complete the project alone, how tired she was of juggling a job along with the restoration? Had the fact that she was still uneasy since the poisoning and thus was not sleeping well become that noticeable?

"Emily?" Simon prodded, reaching across the table and placing his hand over hers. "Please don't fly off the handle or start feeling threatened. You can use the help—you need the help. There's so much I know, so many ways I could help you, show you how to make the work go faster, look more professional." He smiled a little when she bristled. "You've done an outstanding job, honey, but admit it. You *are* an amateur."

"I was going to give in gracefully," Emily grumbled, "but if you're going to adopt that kind of superior stance you can take your help and stuff it in one of the corners you keep poking in for that dumb will." They stared at each other for a minute, then both broke into relieved laughter.

"I was afraid you'd go for my shin bone," Simon confessed between chuckles.

"Well, I'm *still* afraid you're going to bulldoze over my feeble efforts, and then I will go for your shins."

Simon had no difficulty reading between the lines. "Emily," he promised softly, all laughter fading away, "until I find the will, and until the court says so, this house is yours, and Aunt Iris can foam at the mouth all she wants. I only want to help you and enjoy practicing my vocation for the sheer pleasure of doing so. Will you believe me?"

"I'd like to. But Simon, what if you *never* find the will? You've been looking for a month now, and I know conducting business long distance isn't healthy even with all your fancy equipment. How much longer can your great-aunt force you to keep looking?"

Simon stood up, moved around to Emily, and drew her to her feet. "I don't care if it takes the rest of the year." His hands moved warmly from her wrists up to her shoulders. "When are you going to realize that's only an excuse to be near you?"

"What do you mean?" Emily whispered, the question ending in a breathless squeak as he held her close and trailed soft kisses from her temple to her cheek.

"I mean," he murmured, "that I'm tired of pretending that I don't have any feelings. You've flitted around and struggled to feather your nest and chirped on about that lawyer you work for—and not once have you picked up on the fact that I happen to be very attracted to you. *You*, Emily Carson—not the house." He lifted his head, holding his mouth poised just over Emily's. "So...what do you have to say about that?"

Just before her eyes closed, Emily watched the teasing green glitter in Simon's eyes flare into something altogether different. Then he was kissing her, not with the almost angry passion of the first time, but with an exquisite blend of tenderness and restrained desire.

They broke apart abruptly when Samson jumped up onto the chair and meowed, causing Simon to start and pull away from Emily. She sank bonelessly into the chair, automatically picking Samson up as she did so.

Simon laughed shortly, his mouth quirked in wry acknowledgment. "Yes, you striped and whiskered fleabag, you do have some competition for the lady's affections."

"He doesn't have fleas. He's wearing a flea collar," Emily responded with splendid irrelevance. She was spinning, feeling like a playful fall breeze suddenly swirled into a full blown hurricane. Brown eyes wide, dark, and lambent, she gazed up at Simon, struggling to comprehend what had happened.

Simon flexed his shoulders, sighed, and touched her cheek with the tips of his fingers. "Don't look so confused. This has been coming on since the first time I kissed you." He scrutinized her dazed features in something close to exasperation. "Don't tell me you haven't felt the tension between us, Emily, even if I have tried to keep mine under control."

"I felt it," Emily replied very low. "I just had no idea you would feel so...so strongly...."

"You really have no awareness of yourself as an attractive woman, do you?" He raked his fingers through the thick waves of his hair in consternation. "You've mentioned as much before, but I suppose I didn't really believe it. I thought the reason you look the way you do was circumstances more than anything else."

Some of the dazed look sparked into resentment. "And what is that supposed to mean? I can't help it if I'm not a nubile teenager with the seductive charms of Aphrodite."

Simon threw back his head and laughed, a deep, attractive laugh designed to capture and hopelessly tangle heartstrings. "Ah, Emily, what am I going to do with you?" He pondered her now with the old teasing affection, and Emily felt fingers of red creeping up into her cheeks. "Put Samson down."

"What?"

Looking as if he were lifting a smelly bag of garbage, Simon reached and gingerly picked up the cat and deposited him on the floor. Then he once again drew Emily to her feet. "You have something far more beautiful than a seductive figure and alluring manner, Emily Carson," he crooned in soft rhythmic syllables, his hands cupping her face, the thumbs gently stroking her cheekbones. "You have character. And purity. And an inner beauty that shines out to any man who is astute enough to see beneath the camouflage." Emily's hands had risen to tug at Simon's, but they fell helpless to her sides as he released her, then gently touched her braid. "This lovely hair you keep bound...the style-less clothes that reflect your poor self-image...your make-up free face which gazes so guilelessly and fearlessly out at the world and never reveals how lonely and unhappy you are...."

His fingers shushed her as she tried to protest. "You might have convinced yourself and everyone else that you're a contented, quiet lady who could never stir even a ripple of passion in a man, but you're wrong." He smiled into her eyes. "And you know it now, don't you?"

Emily was saved by the bell, literally. The phone rang, and she flung herself away from Simon and scampered down the hall to her bedroom.

"Em? Brad here. Sorry I didn't make it back to the office before you left. I've got the date for your hearing and thought you'd like to know."

The blood pumping furiously through Emily's overheated veins chilled to an abrupt standstill. "When?" she managed to ask, then had to reassure Brad that she was all right, just tired, and no, nothing was wrong before he would answer her question.

Simon was waiting at the entrance to her bedroom, leaning against the door jamb with arms folded across his chest. He was scowling, all teasing and tenderness wiped away. "The lawyer, I presume?" he guessed after she hung up, his voice almost, but not quite, hostile.

Emily nodded. "The hearing is set for this Thursday," she recited, and she looked down at her hands, marveling that they were not quite steady. "Ten o'clock. Your great-aunt's lawyer will have notified her, so I guess I'll see both of you in court, as the saying goes."

Simon stared at her across the room, and it was as if a giant chasm had opened between them. "I guess you will," he agreed evenly.

Emily's chin lifted. "And you'll be flying to Connecticut as soon as possible?"

He sighed deeply. "Yeah. Emily," he stopped, a muscle twitching in his jaw. "I'll call you."

"There's no need—"

"There's *every* need!" He bit out the words, then looked as if he wanted to swallow them back. Turning on his heel, he stalked off down the hall, and a second later she heard the door slam.

Emily sank down onto her bed and buried her head in her hands.

That night Emily jerked awake to the sounds of footsteps prowling around outside the house, then up on the porch. This time, except for Ivan and Samson, she was alone.

At first Emily was so frightened she clung to Ivan, holding the struggling, whining dog to her with her hand clamped over his muzzle so he wouldn't bark. It took several terror-filled minutes to comprehend that insanity, and with a sharp little sob, she let Ivan go.

The dog tore off with a series of roaring barks that would have scared the stripes off a tiger. Emily would not let him outside for fear of what might happen, but at least there were no more footsteps, and after thirty minutes of growling and prowling, Ivan finally settled back down. Emily patted his head and told him he was a good dog, but she didn't sleep at all that night, falling only into a light doze around dawn when the only sound she had heard for hours was Ivan's quiet breathing.

First thing in the morning, she called the county sheriff and explained what had happened. The sheriff dispatched a deputy who tramped around the yard and poked about the porches searching for clues or signs of forced entry. He found nothing. After patting Emily on the shoulder and remarking kindly about women and their generally excitable constitutions, the slightly paunchy, slightly pompous patrolman left. So that day, instead of working on the house, Emily attached a leash to Ivan and embarked on a hike around the parameters of her property. Someone might be using her property for nefarious purposes, and as usual it was up to Emily to take care of the matter.

Gray skies hung like a damp, dirty sheet low and heavy

in the sky. September usually wasn't as hot as August, but the humidity was still high enough to be cloying. The air was ripe with the pungent odor of vegetation and wet earth, but at least the wind was in the right direction to keep the paper mill fumes at bay.

Emily marched across the weed-infested field, intent on starting her investigation at a camping site she and Ivan had happened on one day. She kept Ivan leashed because she could not depend on him to stay close enough for her to protect. A detached part of herself laughed at the irony. Ivan was supposed to be protecting *her*, not the other way around! Simon would definitely not understand.

She would not think about Simon right now. She would not. She would concentrate on searching for signs in her woods that should not be there—beer cans, a campfire—Emily didn't know what she was looking for, but she also knew if she stayed holed up in her house like a sniveling coward afraid of her own shadow, she would never forgive herself.

She tramped for hours through underbrush dripping with dew and the rain from two days ago, beneath silent, slender pine trees whose needles carpeted the forest floor. For awhile she followed the firebreak, but after sidetracking into the woods to search over the abandoned campsite she and Ivan had discovered in July, Emily struck off into the woods on the other side of the little clearing. Stumbling onto an old logging road made walking easier, but Emily had no idea where it would lead. She checked her watch and decided to follow it no more than thirty minutes, since by then she would doubtless have reached the limits of her property anyway. Someday, God willing, she would have to scratch up the funds to have the boundaries surveyed and updated.

The rutted, overgrown road wound through another quiet glade of pines, then meandered about the edge of a huge cleared meadow. Emily decided it was time to start back just as Ivan growled deep in his throat, then emitted a soft warning woof.

Startled, Emily turned, her eyes scanning the field and widening in astonished disbelief. Ivan barked again, louder this time, and with panicked swiftness Emily clamped her hand around his muzzle.

Unbelievably, parked at the far end of the field was a plane. It was small, without the bright colors tipping the tail and wings or body. There was a van beside it, and several men were taking boxes out of the plane and loading them into the van. For a frozen second Emily couldn't move, couldn't think, couldn't even breathe. Drugs. It had to be drugs. It seemed beyond comprehension that she had stumbled onto such a scene, but she had, and all the seemingly isolated incidents of the last months blended together to paint a deadly scenario.

Cars slowing and idling outside her house in the dead of night. A crashed and abandoned car full of cocaine and pornographic materials. The footsteps last night. Had her house—abandoned for years—been used as a drop-off point? Storage for their filthy cargo?

Emily had attributed the mess she had cleaned up when she moved in to relatively harmless hoboes. Now she wasn't so sure.

Ivan struggled, whining, and Emily felt the hair rise on the back of her neck. She had spotted the plane—but that meant they could also see *her*.

Emily grabbed Ivan's collar while her other hand

stayed clamped about his mouth, then turned and as quietly as she could, crept back into the covering of trees. When the shadows of the pines and a curve in the road provided a modicum of safety, she ran, clenching Ivan's leash in a death grip.

She ran until her lungs ached and a stitch in her side doubled her over so that she had to stop and rest. Ivan whined and licked her face. He wasn't even breathing hard, but sat by her panting easily, tongue dripping, waiting for his mistress to tell him what to do next. For one whirling moment Emily thought she was hopelessly lost, but as her labored breathing slowed, she caught the faint sound of the creek. Still breathing in hard stabbing gasps, she stumbled through the woods until they came to the lazily flowing stream and followed it until they reached familiar territory.

Her immediate instinct was to grab the phone and call the police. Even in the process of dialing she hesitated, then slowly replaced the phone in the cradle. Was there any chance they'd believe her after the attitude displayed toward her this very morning by that deputy? Even if they did, Emily doubted she could retrace her path to the field. The plane would have left hours ago, and the van with its deadly load would be on its way to ruin more lives.

Emily pummeled her fists on the wall in frustration and despair. What could she do? She had had first-hand experience of what happened when a person got messed up in drugs, for she and a fellow teacher had caught two ninth graders smoking pot under the bleachers the previous spring, and when their lockers were searched, crack was discovered. One of those boys had been an honor student, with his whole life ahead of him. Now—

Emily picked up the phone again, willing to make a fool of herself for the sake of all the other school kids. Then another, even more unpleasant thought struck: If the police went nosing around the area and found nothing, the jerks who were involved with the trafficking would probably know who had set the authorities on their trail.

She spent the rest of the afternoon and evening sanding kitchen cabinets, but the sweaty, backbreaking labor could not drown out the clamoring voices in her head, all telling her to do something different. So she ended up doing nothing at all. She spent another sleepless night—this time with the hammer by her bed as well as Ivan.

At least she had Ivan. When Simon returned, he and his aunt would be guests of Lamar Hansell, Iris's lawyer, so Emily could *not* depend on Simon's help anymore. That was okay by her. She wasn't stupid—and she had Ivan.

Tomorrow at work, maybe, just maybe, she could talk to Brad and ask him for advice.

Unfortunately, no matter what she decided, she still might end up in a burlap sack at the bottom of the creek, and Iris Bancroft could have the property free and clear, will or no will.

eight

Wednesday morning, Emily dragged herself to work. Brad, chewing furiously on a couple of sticks of spearmint, barely spared her a second glance.

"Hi, Em. Glad you made it. You need to cancel all my morning appointments. Sorry about this. Re-arrange them for...," he chewed even more furiously as he flipped through several pages of notes, his normally pleasant features distorted in a harried scowl. "For Friday, if you can. If they're going to be dead before then, have them come in as late this afternoon as you can—not before four."

He slapped the papers down and muttered something mildly profane, then apologized to Emily. "I have to go to Albany. Gloria left the reminder on my calendar, but she forgot to tell you so you could remind me of the note she left to remind me."

They grinned at each other. Emily was genuinely fond of Brad, for he was an easy person to like. He had been patient with her rusty secretarial skills, had praised her re-organization of his jumbled files, and never failed to remind her that her own case would turn out all right. Emily waved him out the door.

A little while later the secretary for Lamar Hansell called, and nebulous thoughts of drug dealers and death threats vanished from Emily's mind. Tomorrow. This time tomorrow the waiting and wondering would all be over.

What would the judge decide? Were Iris and her lawyer as confident as Brad that *they* would be the "winners"?

How could anybody really win when either Iris or Emily would be devastated, whatever the outcome?

Over the past weeks at odd moments, Emily actually found herself praying for God's help. She even talked to her minister, Sam Noland, as Brad had suggested, marginally relieved when he provided her with some scriptural comfort. According to Pastor Sam, the apostle Paul flat out told the Romans they must submit themselves to the governing authorities—which was what Emily was trying to do now. A lawsuit offered the only alternative to determine legal ownership of the property. Emily's true trial, and manifestation of her Christian faith, would be accepting the outcome graciously.

Brad called at a quarter to five to apologize for not returning in time to go over the procedure for the next day with her. Emily tried to sound offhand, but Brad was too good a lawyer to be misled by her manufactured cheerfulness.

"Don't sound so worried," he counseled her kindly. "It's a fairly straightforward case without the will, Emily. By noon you can go celebrate." There was a pause, then he added hopefully, "Maybe I'll take off a couple of hours and celebrate with you."

Emily found herself wondering what Simon would think about that, so she told Brad with deliberate sweetness that she would love to celebrate with her favorite lawyer. Simon would have his hands full comforting his battle-ax of a great-aunt anyway.

Thursday morning dawned a hot, cloudless day with a brassy sky promising rain by nightfall. Emily dressed carefully, remembering Simon's words concerning her appearance.

Her best, most sophisticated outfit was a suit, bought two years ago for the end-of-the-year PTA banquet. A lovely shade of cinnamon, Emily bought it because it fit okay and had been on sale. She never considered the fact that it turned her into a monochromatic symphony, serving to reflect the truth of Simon's favorite nickname for her.

Her suit teamed with a jewel neck ivory blouse, hair carefully brushed, braided and bound on top of her head, Emily dismally surveyed herself in the mirror. She'd wanted to look brisk and businesslike. But her mirror said she resembled a plain brown sparrow.

Would Simon be there? She had been astonished to find a postcard from him waiting in her mailbox yesterday afternoon, since he'd only been gone two days.

"See you Thursday," Simon had penned in a loose but neat script. "Don't worry about Iris. I'll take care of you, too. So will the Lord—go read Psalm 84:3-4. See you soon, sparrow-girl."

Emily tossed the card in the basket with the ones from her mother and forgot about it.

Brad met her on the courthouse steps, told her she looked fine, then spent the next fifteen minutes alternately explaining the procedure and reassuring his apprehensive client.

"You act like you've been indicted for violating the Controlled Substances Act or something," he teased, attributing Emily's sudden jerk of dismay to more nerves. He wrapped a comforting arm around her shoulders, fished in his pants pockets, and pulled out a stick of wintergreen gum. "Here. That ought to help soothe the savage beast within."

The awful moment passed, and Emily managed not to blurt out her onerous knowledge of a plane loaded with some of those controlled substances. Then the door to the waiting room opened, and Mr. Hansell, Simon, and the smallest woman Emily had ever seen walked through.

At first glance, Iris Bancroft did not look as if she could possibly be Attila the Hun in a ninety-five pound package, as Simon had suggested. Silver hair styled in tight curls framed a lined, mahogany-tanned face devoid of makeup save two bright splotches of rouge on each parchment cheek. One gnarled, bony hand supported her slight weight on a cane while the other rested on Simon's bent arm. She was wearing a severely tailored street dress of a soft mauve color that, Emily admitted, was infinitely more becoming on Iris than Emily's own brown suit was on her. The hand-crocheted collar seemed to emphasize her age and fragility until she opened her mouth.

"So you're the unprincipled, land-grabbing opportunist trying to steal my property."

Simon groaned and the lawyer, who had shut the door behind them, smiled in weary resignation.

"Aunt Iris," Simon reminded the woman quietly but firmly, "the matter is going to be decided legally, and name-calling merely detracts from your own credibility."

Iris bridled at the reproof. She removed her hand from his arm and stumped over to where Emily and Brad were standing, flinty gray eyes fastened on Emily.

"I don't care if you're Cinderella," she snapped, her voice raspy, but clear and strong. "That house is mine." She turned and shook the cane at Simon. "You promised you'd find the will and kick the upstart baggage out, and all you've done is let her make mush of your brains." She expelled a forceful sigh, then concluded, "I always told your mother you were a stubborn, willful brat. Seems to me you haven't changed much."

"Maybe we should wait in the hall," Lamar Hansell suggested hastily.

Simon came up beside his great-aunt and laid an arm about her narrow, bony shoulders. "That won't be necessary," he promised, green eyes measuring Brad's close proximity to Emily. His mouth thinned, something primitive and raw flashing through his eyes. "Now that my aunt has vented her spleen, she'll behave with utmost propriety."

Iris snorted, then swatted Simon's arm. "Don't try to put me in my place, nephew. There's not a man alive capable of doing that!"

The two lawyers suppressed smiles, and everyone moved to sit down in some of the uncomfortable, wooden chairs scattered about the room. Brad had not missed the look in Simon's eye, and he discreetly chose a chair two seats away from Emily. She wanted to swat Simon like Iris had.

They spent a few minutes chatting in restrained, civil fashion, while Iris sat in queenly disdain and ignored them all. But Emily had seen a frightened glitter in her eyes, and when she took a dainty handkerchief from her purse, her hands were trembling. Emily was wretched.

Just before their case was called, Marylou Thomlinson, Mildred Davis's mother and partner, strode into the room, looking like an older copy of Mildred. She had the same brisk energy, the same tall, well-toned body and air of assurance.

"Sorry I'm late," she apologized with a smile encompassing everyone. "Will this take long, Lamar? I need to show a house at noon."

High noon, Emily found herself thinking with crazy humor. All they needed was the music and Gary Cooper. It would all be over by noon.

She only looked at Simon once, as they were all entering the courtroom. He was holding the door for everyone, and as Emily passed through with Brad at her elbow, Simon sliced her a look that would have frozen a welder's blowtorch. Emily couldn't conceal her pained confusion, and his mouth briefly softened. He and Brad exchanged glances, then Brad ushered her to her seat.

What had happened to the Simon who had promised to take care of her?

The procedure lasted only forty-five minutes. The lawyers presented their respective cases, and then the judge retired to his chambers to evaluate the claims before he made his decision. Emily knew he had already studied the case. She just hoped he would make his decision instead of delaying, which Brad had told her was a possibility for which she should prepare herself.

She had *not* been prepared for Marylou Thomlinson's revelations.

According to Mildred's mother, some twenty-six years ago—the very first year she received her broker's license—a man named Harold deCourier had come to see her. He was old and ill, with a very unusual request: He wanted Marylou to handle his father's property—the VanCleef estate—but according to the terms of his father's will, the property could not be sold out of the family for one hundred years from the date of that will.

Harold was, he informed Marylou with touching

shame, VanCleef's illegitimate son, which was why his last name was that of his mother. The time limit would now be up in one more year. Twenty-six years ago Marylou had simply signed an agreement, then filed the whole thing in the back of a drawer, figuring she would probably never sell the property so why worry about it?

She had truly forgotten the whole affair. Over the years, the old deCourier place just sat and rotted out in the country. Harold had died years ago. He had never married and left no will that anyone could find, so there the house sat.

Marylou never told Mildred. Why should she, since she never thought about it? Thus, Brad meticulously proved, Mildred sold Emily the property in good faith.

Emily listened in growing horror and consternation, especially since Iris Bancroft turned out to be the granddaughter of Everett VanCleef, and therefore the legitimate heir. At one point Emily glanced toward the older woman, sitting straight and dignified across the room. No emotion showed on the aging, aristocratic face, but Emily still felt like an unprincipled carpetbagger. She couldn't help it. Once Simon had asked if she would give up the house without a fight. She understood now why Iris was just as determined, and the knowledge was suffocating.

The judge returned, everyone rose, and Emily found that she couldn't take a deep breath. Ten minutes later it was over—and Emily had won. Because the will had not been found and because Harold had died without issue, the judge declared Emily's ownership more legally binding than the terms of the agreement between Harold deCourier and Marylou Thomlinson. Lamar Hansell and Brad shook hands, and Lamar went over to console Iris, who was sitting as if turned to a pillar of salt.

Simon bent over her, whispering, but as Emily and Brad started to leave the room, he straightened and met them at the door. "I'd like to speak to you, Emily."

Brad lifted a tawny brow. When Emily nodded and managed to reassure him with a facsimile of a smile, he murmured that he would wait for her in the hall and left.

"I'm truly sorry for your aunt," Emily told Simon. "Seeing her in action, I can understand why you've had such a time of it." She paused, then added painfully, "Why didn't you explain to me?"

"I only found out Marylou's story two days ago. She was in the Mediterranean all summer, remember? Then too, Aunt Iris believes in playing her cards close to her chest." He regarded her unsmilingly. "Especially now that she knows how I feel about you."

Emily digested those words in stony silence. "And how would that be?" she finally ventured. "From the looks you've thrown my way ever since you walked into the waiting room, I'd about decided I must have turned into the wicked stepmother instead of Cinderella."

A wicked glint appeared briefly. "I did warn you about her tongue, didn't I? At least you haven't had to listen to it for almost three months." The glint disappeared. "What's Lauderman to you, anyway, Emily? Besides your lawyer and employer, that is."

Emily stiffened. "You have no right to ask me such a question. And now that the house is mine...," she faltered, her gaze going in spite of itself to Iris, "twice over, I imagine you'll be going back to your own life."

"And prove I'm as undependable, as faithless, as everyone else in your life?" Simon asked, very softly. When

Emily's eyes jerked back to his, startled, dark, and vulnerable, he lifted his hand and touched her cheek. "You might have your property, but there's still some goings-on to be cleared up, aren't there? Besides—you haven't learned about God's faithfulness yet. I've decided He's appointed me as His representative in your behalf, so get used to the fact that you'll be seeing a lot of me in the future." He opened the door and held it for her. "See you soon."

Emily ate lunch with Brad, but only because he insisted. Before they parted, Brad grasped her arm and waited until he had her full attention. "Emily, I wouldn't be worth the paper my degree was printed on if I didn't warn you about a couple things."

Alarm filled Emily's face, but she relaxed a little when Brad gave her a wide, sheepish smile.

"Sorry. Maybe I should have phrased it in legal jargon. What I mean is that there is every possibility Iris is going to pursue the matter, which means she'll still try and produce the will. If it's found, you'll find yourself being served with your own lawsuit."

"Oh."

"And that brings me to my other warning." He loosened his tie, then crammed his hands in his pants pockets. "Be careful with Balfour. The man has his eye on you, Emily, and it isn't just because of your property."

Emily colored. "It's nothing serious, Brad. I'm not the sort of woman to inspire a man to launch a thousand ships for me. And regardless of what you may think, it *is* the house he's interested in." She smiled a little. "He just has a bee in his bonnet about teaching me a lesson about God."

"What?" Brad laughed suddenly, and shook his head.

"I've heard a lot of lines, but that one takes the cake. He might talk as pretty as a preacher, honey, but that's not what he's got on his mind. I'm a man, and I know." He eyed her thoughtfully a moment, and shrugged. "I entertained a few thoughts myself until I saw which way the wind blew. Go on home, Emily, but keep what I said in mind."

Men, Emily decided as she drove the twelve miles home, were as undecipherable as they claimed women were. As she turned onto the dirt lane her spirits perked up a little. She was sorry for Iris, bemused and irritated by Brad and Simon, but she finally had a home. A home of her own. And now she could relax and get on with the rest of her life.

She had taken Samson in to Dr. Moffat the evening before for his neutering operation. Now the first order of the day was to call and make sure her cat was okay. Shaking her head and chiding herself for forgetting to go by after she left Brad, she also decided to take Ivan for a walk since she had left him inside this morning.

"Hope he didn't chew up anything else," she spoke aloud, feeling the accumulated hours of worry and tension sloughing off her back as if she were shedding a burdensome extra skin. "Poor baby. Maybe I better let him stay outside again. If he's learned—" The words died in her throat.

Jerking to a halt and flinging herself from the car, she ran to the edge of her yard and stared across the field, horror turning to desperation and spiraling fear. The flames were small as yet, but deadly, creeping with scorching fingers in a steady line across the field toward her house. Smoke curled and billowed in gray swirls, and the air had borne it aloft so that it filled her nostrils with the sharp, acrid scent.

Without wasting another second, Emily whirled and raced for the house. Her fingers shook so badly it took three tries to dial the emergency number. Thank God she had a phone now and Ivan was here in the house, Samson safe at the vet's! She tried to calm the whining, worried dog as she explained the situation in a trembling voice to the calm man at the other end of the line. She managed to give directions, then hung up and began tearing her suit off in a panicked frenzy. The fireman had told her to evacuate and move herself and her car to the main highway, but Emily had no intention of sitting by and watching her property go up in smoke.

Yanking on jeans and a dressy, long-sleeved blouse she normally wore to church, ripping a nail as she struggled into socks and tennis shoes, Emily's mind raced as she tried to figure out ways to cap and destroy the flames. Carrying a bucket would be useless—like spitting in the wind. Should she try digging a firebreak? Starting backfires as firefighters did to combat forest fires? Hose down her yard to dampen everything?

She snatched one of J.J.'s old baseball caps she had saved and stuffed it over her hair to keep the braid up out of the way. Grabbing Ivan, she leashed him and then dumped him in her car in case the worst happened. "You'll be safe here," she patted his head, ran her hand briefly but soothingly over his quivering flanks. "I'll be back as soon as I can."

Stumbling and tripping, she ran across the field with a shovel in one hand and a wet rag to tie across her face in the other, sending up incoherent pleas to God, the firemen, Simon, and anyone else she could think of who might help. There was no way she could put out a fire alone, even though she was determined to try.

Sometime later she heard the keening of the fire engines, but she was too busy to be relieved. Smoke stung her eyes and burned her nose, heat scorched and blistered her face and hands as she dug into the earth and flung heavy shovelfuls over the flames; dug and flung until her back was on fire like the field and her hands were raw with sweat and blisters. She was much too preoccupied to notice a sinister figure creeping stealthily out from the woods behind her.

The blow caught her at the back of her neck. She went down like a pine sapling felled by a single swipe of the ax. When the fire engines pulled up five minutes later, there was no sign of Emily.

Consciousness returned by degrees, each more uncomfortable than the last. Her first sensation was the awful, searing pain in her head and neck. On the heels of that revelation came the awareness that she was being carried, flung over someone's shoulder like a bag of fertilizer. She tried to move, to scream, then the third realization that she was bound up inside some sort of sack hit her. She was effectively as helpless as a chicken tossed into the gunny sack of a chicken thief.

After awhile, the labored breathing of whoever was carrying her altered to gasps and grunts of exertion, and she decided somewhat fuzzily that he must have been carrying her a long time because she wasn't *that* heavy. She was on the edge of passing out again when she was unceremoniously dumped onto the ground.

"It's about time," a muffled voice complained testily.

"Put a lid on it," was the sharp reply. "She might look

like a skinny school brat, but you try carrying her on *your* back for forty minutes."

"Don't see why we couldn't just leave her in the field."

"Because that's a murder rap, you dumb scum! Orca made his feelings plain—or are your eyeballs so fried you didn't catch his reaction after that ball-up with Frank and Pete."

"Back off, Gumshoe." The voice came closer, and Emily's heart rose in her throat and tried to suffocate her. "Can we at least have a little fun with the dame? She's not much of a looker, but—"

Emily tried to close her ears to the spate of foul language that followed between the two. She tried to lick her lips, but she was dry-mouthed, parched with fear and thirst and the exertion of fighting the fire. The fire! *Oh, please, God, let the firemen get there on time.*

She wanted to struggle, to free herself from the blinding, scratchy burlap sack that kept her trussed up and helpless. Some deep-seated instinct of survival kept her still, the subconscious voice warning her that movement of any kind would only draw unwelcome attention to her.

But she had to do something. She couldn't just tamely submit to her fate. It wasn't right. It wasn't fair. Never had she felt so helpless, so out of control. Even when J.J. had been at his most rebellious, she at least had been able to talk him into listening to her point of view. And when Mom and Daddy left, she had had the freedom to make a new home. When Simon came and tried to take it away from her she had been able to fight back.

Now she was utterly and completely at the mercy of these thugs, and with that realization she fell into the darkest, blackest pit of despair in the universe. This must have been what Jonah felt like when he had been swallowed by the big fish. What had Jonah done to get out? Emily's conscious mind was coming and going now, flickering in and out like a bad camera reel of a thirties film. Jonah and the whale...sparrows...Simon called her sparrow-girl because of that song...a song about a whale? No, it had something to do with God...His eye is on the sparrow. That was it...Jonah had prayed and up out of the fish he came. But he was a man and she was just a sparrow-girl...God wouldn't listen to her prayers..."His eye is on the sparrow, and I know He watches me...."

Help me, Lord. Send Simon before it's too late....

nine

Emily was picked up again, roughly, and dumped with scant ceremony into the seat of some kind of vehicle. Through a semi-conscious daze, she heard a new voice speaking in a high-pitched whisper.

"Hurry! They got the fire out and now they're looking for the girl!"

"Did you take care of that mutt?"

After a horrible pause the third voice replied in a grudging tone: "Yeah. I...took care of him."

Emily didn't notice the bouncing ride or the pounding pain in her head. Tears dripped down her cheeks, soaking her face as, heartsick, she grieved for her innocent pet. He had been slaughtered because she hadn't gone for help when she had the chance.

Ivan was dead, and she was probably next on the list, no matter what that other man said.

After awhile, they pulled onto a smoother road, and the bouncing and bumping ceased. The car picked up speed, but Emily had no sense of where they were or which way they were going.

Fortunately, the drive didn't take long. With a squealing of tires and a jolting turn that threw Emily against the door, the car jerked to a halt. Gravel voice—had he been called Gumshoe?— cursed the driver roundly, then Emily heard doors wrenched open, and she was hauled out feet first and once again slung over a shoulder.

She sensed the presence of the other two men walking

on either side. She could hear multiple footsteps, smell the malodorous combination of sweat, cigarettes, and unwashed bodies.

"This is far enough," one of them finally whined. "It'll take her until tomorrow to find her way back as it is. Let's split, man. I don't like this."

Suddenly Emily was yanked off the shoulder and then held suspended by two hands grinding into her arms like giant metal braces.

"I hope this little scare will teach you to keep your nose out of business that don't concern you. Next time we won't be so *gentle*." There was a harsh bark of laughter. "You might end up in the same shape as your dog." The clamps suddenly released her and she collapsed onto the ground. "Nice meeting you, Ms. Carson. If you value your hide and that pile of bricks, you better not venture too far out of it into the woods anymore."

Emily struggled weakly to lift the stifling cloth, but that crunching vise of a hand stayed her movement. "I don't want to see you move until we're long gone, lady. And for the sake of your continued health, forget what you saw in the meadow the other day."

The sound of the footsteps retreated. A short while later the car engine roared to life and gunned off down the road. Emily was alone.

Silence lapped over and around her, gently lifting her up out of the dark hole and tugging at her dazed senses. Eventually she moved her hands and fumbled weakly with the corner of the sack, managing after several abortive attempts to tug it over her head. She winced as the late afternoon sun struck her eyes. How could this possibly still be the same day? Had it only been this morning that she'd learned she was the bona fide, one-and-only legal owner of that...pile of bricks? Shock and grief and a residue of terror stiffened her spine, and she forced herself to stand. It took a couple tries.

"What a mess..." Emily mumbled, her voice a quavering husky croak.

In the distance, she heard the faint drone of a plane, the plaintive call of a bird, a car. A car? Feeling like the scarecrow from *The Wizard of Oz* whose stuffing was scattered all over the field, Emily dragged herself a few steps, swaying and dizzy and trembling. They hadn't carried her very far that last time. Hopefully the road was close by.

She fought a stumbling, wavering path through waist high goldenrod and milkweed, and prayed. Even though she was neither starving, nor a prisoner of war, nor dying of cancer, she hoped under these particular circumstances the Lord might incline His ear for a few minutes, if only until she were safely home.

The road proved to be an ancient county road, paved in the distant past with asphalt that was now cracked and crumbling, with weeds encroaching on the edges. If she were lucky, another car might pass by before next week. For the first time since she had been released, Emily's chin trembled. It was one thing to keep your sense of proportion when your life was on the line—it was another thing entirely when you were spared, but then were solely responsible for your continued well-being.

Simon. If only he were here. He would know what to do. He would take care of her. What was she thinking? She could take care of herself, as she had always done. She couldn't depend on anyone, including Simon Balfour. This was the man whose great-aunt wanted her home, who would doubtless be after Simon to keep on looking for the will regardless of this morning's outcome.

Iris Bancroft reminded Emily of the story in the Bible about the widow who kept nagging the judge until he gave her what she wanted, just to be rid of her. From what she had seen and heard of the elderly woman, the judge who this morning had ruled in Emily's favor might eventually reverse his decision just to get rid of Iris.

Simon would have his hands full with his great-aunt. He also had his own life to consider. Surely his team of specialists couldn't do *all* the restoration work in his absence; if they could, they'd go into business for themselves.

Besides, she had made it plain she wasn't interested. All that talk about being God's emissary was nothing but talk, just like Brad tried to warn her. Men were a strange lot, but it was not in Emily to figure them out right now. She had all she could do to put one foot in front of the other and find out if there were a phone or a house at the end of this winding little road.

A sunburned, dust-covered farmer driving a tractor pulling a flatbed of hay came upon Emily a half hour later. He helped her up, and she lay in the warm, sweet smelling hay as the farmer urged the ancient chugging tractor to its limit.

The farmer's wife exclaimed over her, put her on a couch, and nursed her with hot tea. Then she was driven to the county hospital, where an extremely large, comfortable-looking nurse clucked over her smoke- and dirt-laden state. A doctor examined her and harrumphed a lot, but he refused to tell her anything. Emily was wearily trying to remember the name of her insurance agent in Sylvan to tell the nurse when the curtain shielding her from the other cubicles in the small emergency room was flung wide.

Simon erupted into view, his body a coiled spring of tension and his eyes wild. "Emily, are you all right?...Emily!"

"Sir," the nurse tried to protest in her best matronly tone, "you can't come in here right now—"

Simon did not budge. "I can and I have." He was at Emily's side immediately, his hand reaching out with trembling fingers to touch her cheek, still red from fighting the fire. "Emily." He couldn't seem to say anything else and stood gazing down at her with red-rimmed eyes. Emily stared back. "Simon...." She passed her tongue over her cracked lips. "How did you find me?"

For a minute his eyes closed as if in agony, and his hands clenched the side of the table with such force the knuckles gleamed white. "I drove out to see you—the firemen were just putting out the last of the flames. Your car was there, but no one had seen you."

He picked up her hand and held it, caressing her fingers, then lifted it to his lips. "We searched everywhere. Someone found an old baseball cap with some of your hairs attached, and your shovel, but that was it." He looked down at her with such naked pain that Emily was shocked out of her *own* pain and exhaustion. "I never want to go through those feelings again. I called the police, Barb and Taylor, Lauderman...."

For the first time, the glimmer of a smile lightened his face. "Do you realize there are probably fifty or so people and officials in two counties combing the woods around your property for you? When the hospital notified the sheriff that a young woman fitting your description had been brought in, I burned up the road getting here."

Emily licked her dry, cracked lips. "I had no idea anyone would go to so much trouble," she whispered.

"How badly are you hurt?" he asked abruptly. "Can I take you home? Are you going to be up to answering some questions from the police—and me?"

"I'm all right. Mostly shaken...and a headache. The doctor hasn't really filled me in...." Her voice faded and she bit her lip, her gaze dropping to watch her hands fidgeting with her blouse. "Simon...I think I've gotten in over my head this time...."

His hand covered both of hers and stilled the agitated movements. "Whatever happened is not as important as the fact that I've got you here, now, and you're safe." He drew in a deep breath and his hand tightened reassuringly. "Were you assaulted, Emily?"

The question was voiced softly, almost off-handedly, but Emily was not too battered to miss the undercurrents, and suddenly she was as much afraid of what Simon might do as she was of the three thugs who had manhandled her and—and killed Ivan.

"Not exactly," she dragged out unsteadily. "They—I—was being taught a lesson." She tried to take a breath. "Ivan. They...they...." She couldn't go on, but Simon didn't need the words spelled out.

"I'm sorry, Emily." Leaning forward, he brushed his lips comfortingly over her forehead. "I wondered when we couldn't find him and hoped he might be with you." He waited a minute, then prodded in a gentle, coaxing tone, "Who is 'they,' honey?"

"It would have been nice if you'd waited for us, Balfour."

A short stocky man in a khaki sheriff's uniform strolled over to stand at the foot of the gurney. "Miss Emily Carson? I'm Sheriff Travis Jessup. Mighty glad you're okay, ma'am. Some of my men were getting ready to pen this fella here up in a cage—he was about as uptight as a renegade cougar." He hooked his thumbs in his gun belt and surveyed Simon and Emily. "Care to tell us about it, ma'am? Doc Wilburn says you're a mite battered about, but nothing near bad enough to stay unless you really want to."

"No." Emily allowed Simon to help her sit up, dangling her legs on the side of the gurney. "No, I don't want to stay here."

Both men waited in taciturn silence while Emily haltingly related her tale of terror. A time or two, Sheriff Jessup inserted a question, but Simon kept silent. His gaze never left Emily, and the hand holding hers refused to let go.

"And then they left and I made my way to the road, and the farmer—I don't remember his name—found me and brought me here."

"The only names you remember hearing are Frank and Gumshoe and another funny sounding name you can't remember?" the sheriff quoted from his notes, watching Emily intently.

Emily nodded wearily, her head throbbing—her whole body was throbbing. Simon's hand held hers in a warm comforting clasp, however, which tightened when the doctor returned.

"She can go," he repeated, albeit reluctantly. "For the first twenty-four hours she probably ought to be monitored, maybe wake her every couple of hours through tonight—just as a precaution." He glanced from Simon to Emily and back again. "I take it this gentleman will see to those conditions?"

"You take it right."

The doctor winked down at Emily, patted her shoulder, and left. Simon held out his hand to the sheriff. "Thanks for everything. I'll get her settled first and then square things away as to addresses and procedures."

"Sure thing, Mr. Balfour. Miss Carson—I'll be in touch." He scratched his chin, looking uncomfortable. "I'm sorry 'bout all this, ma'am...." He touched his hat, gestured to Simon, and walked out.

Simon smiled down at Emily. "I'll be right back. Don't move."

When he came back a few minutes later, he looked grim, but the hands helping her to her feet handled her with exquisite gentleness. "I'm taking you to Barb and Taylor," he said. "They'll put us up until I can call my folks. By the way, we're going down there as soon as you're up to it."

He helped her walk slowly toward the exit, keeping an arm about her shoulders and matching his stride to hers, talking in a soft, steady patter of words. "The sheriff and I decided whisking you off to Florida until this mess is cleared up a little would be our best option. No—don't shake your head at me. It's all been taken care of.

"Barb is something else, isn't she? When I got in touch with her, I thought she was going to come after me with her food processor—then I thought she was going to collar the FBI director himself if she had to hire a private jet to get there to do it."

Emily tried to laugh. That sounded like Barb.

Simon looked pleased. "She got on the phone and inside of thirty minutes had your entire hometown on its way over to start a search." He eased her into the seat of his Jensen-Healy, and they backed out of a parking spot marked "Ambulances Only," then drove slowly off down the street.

Emily leaned back in the seat, her eyes closing against the steady beat of pain, against the rapid tide sweeping her willy-nilly down a stream she was helpless to paddle against. "I can't go to your parents, Simon."

"Just rest, sparrow-girl. Just rest. I've got you now, and everything's going to be okay."

She rolled her head sideways, being careful not to jar the swollen lump. "Do you really think God has His eyes on sparrows?" she mused in a faraway, fading voice.

"I know He does." His hands clenched suddenly on the wheel, and his voice went rough and raw. "I couldn't have stood it otherwise." And on that note silence reigned.

They spent two nights with the Chakensis family. Barb and Taylor wanted Emily to move in with them, but Simon remained obdurate—the next day he was taking her to his parents' home in Florida. Friends dropped in to ask after her and offer aid and comfort, but the bulk of their advice centered around a central theme: under no circumstances should Emily return to her house.

The police had been unable to find any sign of her abductors, although after hearing Emily's story about the plane, they combed the woods, looking for the open pasture. Emily had not talked to Sheriff Jessup since the day after the fire, so she had no idea if they had found any clues or not.

"I suppose there's at least a smidgen of good in being knocked out and hauled around like a sack of dirty laundry," she commented over supper that evening. "At least my story is taken a little more seriously. Now I'm not just a neurotic woman living alone and scaring myself to death with my imagination."

Simon paused in the act of taking a bite of his mashed potatoes. "Has someone been giving you that impression?"

"Not since I was bashed over the head," Emily provided hastily. Simon was becoming more and more possessive, and it was downright uncomfortable, if not awkward. She had never had anyone fuss over her before, treating her as if she were fragile and needed protecting. Part of her responded as a desert flower responds to spring rains, but the rest of her remained a wary, prickling cactus.

"The man who came out after I heard someone walking around outside the house one night treated me more or less like a feeble minded ninny." She abruptly became aware of three sets of eyes boring holes of recrimination into her and ducked her head guiltily. She had forgotten that they hadn't known about that incident.

"You heard someone walking around outside and didn't say anything?" Barb's voice ended in a shriek, and Mark and Lara put their hands over their mouths and giggled.

"Calm down, honey," Taylor remonstrated his wife before turning to his children and adding sternly, "You two go take your baths and get ready for bed. You've got school in the morning."

"Em, why couldn't you be back teaching? Dump that house and come back here where you belong, where you'll be safe."

Emily very carefully laid her crumpled paper napkin by her plate and rose. "I have a very good job as Brad's secretary," she responded in a colorless monotone, "and as for belonging—I feel more at home in that house with Ivan and—" She stopped as a rush of emotion threatened to engulf her. "Excuse me," she muttered, and fled out into the back yard.

Simon followed her a little while later. She was sitting in a rope swing with a board seat Taylor had rigged for the children, her feet idly scuffing the dirt patch beneath it where all the grass had been worn away. She was staring fixedly into space with a closed, blank expression, but the hands clasping the rough hemp rope as if she were clutching a lifeline betrayed her inner turmoil. Without a word, Simon gave her back a gentle push and began swinging her, his hands warm and firm.

"I could accept it better if they had at least left his body," Emily offered almost inaudibly. "At least I could have buried him and grieved and gotten it over with."

"I know." His hands kept up the gentle pushing, but each time they pressed into her back for that brief instant of contact, they somehow conveyed a message of caring sympathy.

Emily closed her eyes a few minutes to try and savor the early evening and relax. Last night the wind had changed, bringing in a cool front and the deep blue skies of approaching fall. The breeze riffling through her hair with the motion of the swing smelled of dry leaves and smoke and mid-September. In front of her, the sun had just slipped over the horizon, leaving behind a pastel watercolor sky of pale orange and pink and blue.

Life should have been serene, like a happy child

tossing tiny pebbles into a placid pool. But it took everything Emily had to keep from bursting into tears.

"Sunset's beautiful, isn't it?" Simon observed as if he knew Emily needed to change the subject. "I think sometimes that God reveals Himself the most dramatically in sunsets and sunrises, don't you?"

"I suppose."

"But I've also found He can reveal Himself just as dramatically in other ways—sometimes to my cost."

Emily swung up and back, up and back, and then gave in. "What do you mean?" she asked.

She heard Simon chuckle softly. "Sometimes that still small voice we Christians are supposed to cultivate is more of a first sergeant's shout when I'm not listening like I should." He gave her braid a gentle tug as he pushed her away. "Like when I lose my regrettable temper, or when I'm so blind with worry I forget."

"Forget what?" Emily found herself persisting.

Simon stopped the swing and his hands closed over hers. He turned her, swing and all, to face him, holding her not only with his hands but with the compelling message in his eyes. "When I forget the faithfulness of God," he declared with the strength and depth of a mountain stream. "When I try to control all the circumstances, forgetting that He's promised to stay with us at all times—good and bad—so all I really need to do is trust Him to deliver."

ten

Sheriff Jessup met them at Emily's house early the next morning before they took off on the short drive to Florida.

"Got a few leads," he informed them after inquiring after Emily's health and shaking Simon's hand. "We found the field they were using as an airstrip, but needless to say we found nothing else useful. We'll stake it out awhile just in case, though." He glanced around the library. "You did a nice job on this room, but why don't you clean up that window?"

"I'm saving it for last." Emily shrugged self-consciously. "It was sunbeams hitting that window and reflecting on my windshield that brought the house to my attention, and when I discovered the window, I knew I had to have this place."

She sighed. "But it's been a lot harder and more tedious than I dreamed it would be," she slanted a quelling look at Simon, "and imagining how beautiful my window will look when it's cleaned up is all that keeps me going sometimes."

"You've done a first class job," Simon assured her. He nodded toward the window. "I've been itching to get my hands on it myself. I've restored period homes all over the South and have never come across a lead glass window of this caliber in a private residence. I'm pretty sure it's a Tiffany or LaFarge, but since Emily hasn't given me permission to check more closely, I have to suffer in silence." He smiled at Emily's look of astonishment, but now was not the time to pursue the matter.

"Have you found out anymore about the low life creeps who assaulted Emily?"

The sheriff nodded in satisfaction. "Her hearing the name 'Gumshoe' was a piece of luck for us. We've been in touch with the DEA and the FBI, and they both had this character on file." He contemplated his scuffed up shoes a minute, hand stroking his chin.

"I wasn't too wild hearing that—means this is more than a bunch of locals out to make a few fast bucks. Gumshoe is a former private investigator, hence the nickname. His real name is Henry Parskoni. He apparently lost his license because of his cocaine habit—he's street smart and a real cynical son of a gun. He's also careful. I'm surprised he let the mention of his name slip by."

"What about the other guy Emily mentioned?" Simon asked.

"Nothing yet. But we do think we've tied this incident to the wreck that resulted in two casualties back in July."

"My mailman said there was a second car involved, and you had found some drugs inside it."

"Yes'm." He hesitated, then added, "High grade stuff—and two boxes of the most disgustin' porno books and magazines I ever had the misfortune to see." He shook his head slowly, looking every inch the world-weary, battle-worn officer of the law fighting a war he couldn't win. "Whole darn country's straight on a road to hell, if you'll forgive the expression, ma'am. It's the tip of the iceberg down here, since we suspect this area might be one of the drop-off points of a pipeline from South America. We've figured on average, we only manage to seize about fifteen percent of this garbage before it hits the streets." For a minute the three of them struggled with the weight of their helplessness, then Sheriff Jessup put his hat back on and moved briskly toward the front hall. "Well, I'll be going now that I've apprised you of the situation. Let me know twenty-four hours before you bring her back, and I'll assign some men to her."

"Thanks," Simon said. He looked as grim as the sheriff.

"Glad you're feeling okay, Miss Carson. You try to just rest and forget all this." He looked around the room one last time and shook his head again. "It's a shame. A darn shame...."

Emily hastily tossed some clothes in the suitcase Simon had brought in from his car. Barb had packed her some things the other day, but Emily, who had never given much thought to dressing herself up as long as she was fairly neat and clean, found herself wondering what Simon's parents would think of her. Probably as a mousey, colorless woman Simon had taken under his wing for incomprehensible reasons of his own.

As she knelt on the floor of her closet, she tried to bolster her drooping spirits. Why not just look at the experience as an all-expense paid vacation to Florida with a very attractive man? It was too bad she didn't have an address for Mom and Daddy—she could have sent them a postcard.

She pushed her clothes aside and tugged at a box of summer clothes and other stuff she had never unpacked. A corner of the box seemed to be stuck on something, and she pulled harder, wanting to finish and be on her way so she wouldn't have to think anymore about her motivation for giving in to Simon so easily.

There was an ominous sound of ripping wood, and with a muttered exclamation, Emily peered behind the tangle of clothes into the dark interior of the closet. Wonderful. One of the cardboard flaps on the box had caught on a loose panel or something in the wood. She carefully edged her fingers behind the flap and in between the splintering panel to try and disconnect them.

"Just what I need. Something else to repair!" Emily grumped aloud, stifling a sigh of frustration as she tried to feel what was going on. The closet didn't have a light in it, and she didn't feel like searching for a flashlight. With a sudden spurt of impatience, she tugged at the wood and the cardboard flap, scraping her knuckles as she did so.

A tearing, rending sound announced that the wood, as well as the flap, had pulled free of the wall. Emily yanked the box of clothes out of the closet and shoved the clothes on hangers out of the way. She was planning to stuff the displaced panel back, when her fingers encountered something cold and metallic in the space behind it.

The realization of what she had uncovered struck her a stunning blow, and with shaking hands she withdrew what turned out to be a metal strongbox. She backed unsteadily out of the closet and stood, black spots dancing before her eyes.

With a feeling of sick foreboding, she laid the dusty coffer on the floor. Incredibly, it wasn't locked, and after only a slight hesitation, it opened quite easily. Inside was a faded manila envelope, so old it was closed by old-fashioned strings tied around a button. Inside the envelope was a folded sheet of paper, with the heading "Last Will and Testament of Everett VanCleef" written in an elaborate, bold script across the top.

"What's taking so long?" Simon appeared in the doorway. "Emily? What's the matter? What's that?"

He crossed to her side, studying her face, but his gaze dropped to her hands when she mutely held up the will. "Oh, no," Simon breathed, a stillness coming over his body. "Why now?"

With careful fingers, he lifted the will from Emily's trembling hands and began reading aloud, his voice a somber, expressionless baritone. "'I, Everett Peter VanCleef, being of sound mind and declaring this instrument to be my last will and testament, dispose of my properties as follows....'"

"Simon," Emily sighed in a wisp of an undertone, "I feel sort of funny. I think I'd better sit—"

She swayed, then Simon's arm was around her, and he was guiding her over to the bed. They sat down together, and his hand moved to the back of her neck. Pressing with gentle insistence, he made her lower her head almost to her knees.

He kept her there a few minutes while he massaged her neck, being careful with the still tender bruise where she had been hit. "Easy, easy, love," he quieted her with his voice and hand. "I'm sorry...so sorry...."

There was the sound of rustling paper and then his other hand slid beneath her chin and lifted her back up. Emily was incapable of hiding the shock, the inertia of shattering defeat that revealed itself in her stricken eyes.

"I can't bear it," she choked out, her voice still nothing but a thready wisp. "I've lost everything. Everything. I can't bear it anymore."

"Shh...shh. You haven't lost everything, I promise."

Emily very carefully removed herself from his hold and stood up. "Brad warned me if the will were found Miss Bancroft would have a good chance of winning a second lawsuit." Her unseeing eyes fastened on her shoulder bag lying in a jumbled heap on the bed beside the half-filled suitcase. She picked it up, rummaging inside until she found the huge old brass key.

"Here," she held it out to Simon. "Take it. I quit. I can't handle any more. I hope you enjoy restoring it." Her voice drifted off, then resumed in a vague, dreamy tone. "I wonder if Brad could use a full time secretary...." She looked around. "I'll try and move my stuff out as soon as I can."

Simon stood up, and with utmost gentleness took Emily by the shoulders and walked her down the hall into the kitchen. She looked, Simon found himself thinking in agony, even worse than when she had told him about Ivan. *Lord, what can I do? She needs You now more than ever—because I don't know if she'll ever trust me again.*

Sitting Emily down in the kitchen chair, Simon fixed her a glass of water and told her to drink it. After pawing through the largely empty cupboards, he finally unearthed a half-empty box of animal crackers. "I want you to eat these while I finish packing your suitcase," he instructed Emily as he would a child.

Emily looked at the cookies and water. "All right, Simon," she said apathetically, her entire posture speaking so wrenchingly of defeat that it was all he could do to keep himself from grabbing her and wrapping her in a fierce embrace.

He strode back to her bedroom, shoved in the suitcase what few clothes remained to be packed, and slammed the lid shut. If she needed something else, he could buy it for her later, but right now he was determined to clear out and get Emily on the road to Florida.

He glanced around the bathroom, then prowled the downstairs rooms to make sure everything was secure. Jessup had promised to keep an eye on the premises while they were gone, the vet was caring for the cat, and the post office was holding her mail. All Simon had to do was keep Emily from giving up completely.

He laughed a bitter, mirthless laugh. Might be too late for that, he thought, and he couldn't blame her. Why had she had to find that blasted will? For two cents he'd burn the thing and be done with it, but he knew that evasion and lies and pretense were never the answer.

Jaw firming in renewed determination, he returned to the kitchen. "Come on, honey," he glanced at the barely touched water, the box of crackers still in the exact position he had left them. "We'll eat on the way." He put his hand beneath her elbow and tugged her up.

Looking neither at him nor around the house, Emily followed blindly. She was a lifeless, broken doll and her once vibrant, spunky personality lay in a crumpled heap somewhere deep inside her. She allowed Simon to lead her outside and down the steps, then over to the mid-sized sedan he had rented to make the trip more comfortable.

Emily slept most of the trip.

Nathaniel and Katherine Balfour had built a beachfront home years before on a tiny strip of a peninsula at the bottom of Florida's panhandle. Simon spent the bulk of the six-and-a-half hour drive praying while he drove, watching Emily as much as he did the road.

She still looked pole-axed, a docile, passive zombie. Simon would have preferred tears, or even her unpredictable, almost humorous display of temper rather than this present lifeless state. Right now she reminded him of a snuffed out candle.

Barb and Taylor had shed a goodly amount of insight into Emily's complex personality, her paradoxical blend of reckless confidence and the easygoing phlegmatic woman so astonished by her own capacity for passion. As far back as they could remember, Emily had had to pretty much play a lone hand. Her parents should never have had children, Barb contended forcefully, because they were both basically selfish people.

"They never neglected their kids or abused them exactly," she admitted. "It was more like they were just going through the motions of being parents, just waiting till Emily and J.J. were old enough to take care of themselves." She smacked her lips fondly at Taylor, who shook his head at her and returned the blown kiss. "I mean, they dropped her and J.J. off at church, but never went themselves. And if Emily was receiving an award at school or something, her mom would slip in long enough to see Emily, then disappear before it ended so she wouldn't have to go backstage and be around all the other kids. Emily said once that kids make her mother nervous."

"You're making her sound like a cold-hearted monster," Taylor remonstrated mildly.

Barb shrugged her plump shoulders. "You weren't as close to Emily as I was. She used to come over to our house after we became best friends in high school and just sit in the kitchen listening to Mama and me yak. She'd get the most wistful look on her face. Mama used to cry after she went home because she felt so sorry for her."

"I suppose work was sort of a substitute for her," Simon finished, his own heart wrenching as he thought of what Emily had become, and what she could have been had anyone taken the time and care to let her know she was special and loved.

"In a way," Taylor put in, his expression thoughtful. "I also think it was just as much an escape. At home she had indifferent parents and a wild, rebellious younger brother she spent most of her youth keeping out of trouble. At least at work she could be validated somewhat."

Breaking away from his silent reverie, Simon woke Emily as he turned onto the narrow road that ended at the gate of a state park encompassing the northern half of the peninsula. His parents lived a few miles south, and as they would be arriving in less than fifteen minutes, he knew Emily would need some time to compose herself. He also needed a few quiet moments to determine how best to proceed with their relationship.

He pulled the car to the sandy shoulder of the road and shut off the engine. He had known since the day she was abducted that he was more involved emotionally with Emily Carson than he had ever been with another woman—but he was uncertain about the future.

Was he ready to make the kind of commitment required to keep from destroying her? He knew things had reached a point where he would either have to back out of her life completely and take that risk—or be prepared to be bound to her the rest of his life. Did he love her? As if with a mind of its own, his hand slid across the back of the seat to trace a smoke-light path across the crown of her head.

This morning at Barb and Taylor's house—another

age ago—she had meticulously woven her hair into a neat French braid, and Simon had overheard her anxiously asking Barb if she looked respectable enough to meet his parents. His fingers smoothed the silky soft layers, and he had to fight to keep from awakening her with a kiss.

Respectable! *God, I really need your guidance now. If this woman is the one You have chosen to be my mate, I need to know—I need a little more confidence not only with my own feelings, but hers.* He knew Emily still didn't place much trust either in the Lord or him. Actually, she didn't trust *anyone*. And yet he knew that at one time she had accepted Christ for her eternal salvation.

She stirred, head rolling toward him slightly so that the still neat braid slid over his hand and spilled down the seat. Simon fingered the plait, wanting to bury his face in the softness with so urgent a need he had to force himself to move away from Emily completely. He had felt desire before, knew how powerful the sexual drive could be. But never had he felt the tremendous pull when tenderness was coupled with that desire. He wanted Emily with every drop of warm red blood in his body, but he also wanted to protect her, to shield her, to convince her that his feelings for her were more than raw passion.

He flexed his tense shoulders and drew a deep breath. He would definitely have to talk things over with his own parents, who thankfully were the loving, supporting parents God intended a mother and father to be. He bowed his head a minute and sent up his fervent petition, then slid back across the seat.

"Emily." He gave her shoulder a gentle squeeze. "Wake up, love. We're almost there."

Emily lifted heavy-lidded eyes and blinked slowly, dazedly. Lifting her hands, she rubbed her eyes with her knuckles like a sleepy little girl, stretched, and winced at the stiffness of her muscles.

"Here," Simon offered, turning her with careful hands, "I'll massage some of the kinks out for you."

"Where are we?" Emily croaked, her voice still blurred with sleep.

"We're about five miles from my folks' home. You've been asleep over four hours."

"Oh." She sat up straight and twisted back around to face him. Her eyes were wide, very dark. "I wish I could just sleep forever."

Simon scowled. "I made a promise to myself that I wouldn't lose my temper with you anymore, Emily. But if you make any more statements like that, I'll be tempted to change my mind."

"I wasn't talking about suicide," she refuted with indifferent flatness. "I just don't have the energy to face anything or anyone right now."

Simon relaxed, and he gave her braid a tug. "My folks aren't 'anyone,' so you won't be having to face anything except a quiet, deserted beach and the tide tickling your toes. *And* some good Southern cooking to put meat back on your scrawny bones." He re-started the car and drove slowly along the winding asphalt, rolling the window down so they could smell the sea breezes.

"Simon?" Emily ventured in a small voice a few moments later when he turned onto a bumpy lane of shifting white sand and gravel.

He turned his head, his ear caught by the soft uncertainty of her tone. "What, honey?"

"Do you think they'll be angry with me for buying your great- aunt's house and causing so much trouble?"

He winced. "Emily," he ground out with commendable restraint, "*You* are not causing the trouble. You're an innocent victim, on all levels, and nobody blames you for anything. And my parents will love you—exactly as you are."

She turned her head aside, gazing out at the gnarled scrub oaks and pine scrubs and the dunes. It was a surprisingly wild and desolate stretch of land for Florida, but Simon had a feeling right now it matched Emily's mood exactly.

Moments later, his mother threw her arms around him and covered him in flour and laughter and kisses. A spare woman with gray-brown hair and Simon's green eyes, she apologized unrepentantly as Simon tried to fend her off. "I'm making biscuits, but I guess I forgot in the emotion of the moment."

His father hugged him as well, then clasped his hand in a firm handshake. "You're looking good, son." He looked Simon up and down, then his shrewd hazel eyes moved to Emily.

Although not a large man, Nathaniel Balfour had the wiry toughness honed by a life spent outdoors working at physical labor. He was almost bald, and wrinkles crisscrossed his tanned face, giving him more of the weathered look of a farmer instead of the carpenter he had been.

Emily stood quietly off to the side, watching with reserved solemnity while the wandering son was welcomed home. When Simon finally reached to tug her over, he could feel her stiffness, sense the awkwardness as if he were inside her skin.

"You would be Emily." Nathaniel Balfour stepped over to her and held out his hand. His wife elbowed in between and gave Emily another floury hug.

"Don't be so formal, hon," she admonished her husband with a wink to Emily. "Emily will get the wrong impression." She lifted the hem of the faded apron she wore and wiped some flour off Emily's arm. "Emily, welcome to our home. We want you to make it yours for as long as you like." She beamed at Simon with maternal indulgence. "Simon has kept us informed of your miserable state of affairs, and Nat and I feel what you need is a nest right now where you can feel safe and spoiled."

"You can also see if you can put a pound or two on her," Simon chimed in, reaching out a long arm and catching a stiff Emily next to him. "That way when I hold her I know it will be a woman instead of a baby bird."

Emily blushed, and Katherine Balfour gave a delighted peal of laughter. "What a silver-tongued wretch you are," she chided him. "Come on, Emily. I'll show you to your room before I get back to my biscuits. Simon, you and your father can bring in your cases. Supper's at seven, so you should have time to take her for a short walk down the beach."

eleven

Emily followed Mrs. Balfour down a long cool hall, feeling off-balance and strangely shy. This was not the kind of greeting she had steeled herself for, and Simon's parents were...were as nice as Simon himself could be when he chose.

"I hope this will be all right," Mrs. Balfour gestured to the small but light and airy room.

Emily nodded and smiled, but couldn't think of a thing to say. The Balfour home was beautiful but not as elaborate as Emily would have expected. Built on stilts, with a rustic cedar exterior, wraparound porches, and a gable roof with one side extending over the back porches, it was a house to be lived in rather than showcased. Simon had mentioned that his father had built it all himself, disdaining his eldest son's offers of help.

Though not a luxury resort, the house exuded a quiet charm, a welcoming comfort that seemed to reach out gentle hands and tug at Emily's bruised and battered heart. She turned to Simon's mother, struggling to find the words, and found the older woman studying her with such a wealth of compassion that Emily's eyes misted.

Horrified, she walked over to the window and looked out, saying the first thing that occurred to her. "What a wonderful view."

Katherine joined her and laid a work-roughened hand on her shoulder. "Emily, I have three children, and I love them all dearly. They live separate lives with their own families now, but whenever they have a problem, or just need to get away from things, they come here." She patted Emily's shoulder once more and then moved away.

"There's a phrase in the Bible I've always loved—the one hanging on the wall over there." She waited until Emily turned and found the small framed verse on the wall behind the rocker. "'He reached down from on high and took hold of me; he drew me out of deep waters,'" she quoted with lilting softness. "Simon has shared with us some of what you've been going through—I hope you won't mind. Nat and I both pray your being here will help you to feel the Lord drawing you out of those deep waters."

She walked out then, quietly shutting the door behind her, leaving Emily alone.

For a long time Emily stood at the window and watched the waves lifting in white foamy crescents, then ebbing away from the clean sandy shore. If there were any peace this side of heaven, surely one could find it here.

If God were truly in His heaven and all was right with the world everywhere else, would it be asking too much for Him to make things all right in her own little corner of the world? A tear slipped out and dribbled forlornly down her cheek. Simon's parents seemed so nice...so much like, well, like a mother and a father ought to be. No wonder Simon was so confident, so sure that God was taking care of things. He had grown up with a family who seemed to demonstrate that kind of love every day.

From down the hall, Emily could hear the sound of their voices, the deeper bass of Simon's father softening the lilting mezzo-soprano of his mother. And Simon's voice, a mixture of rich black coffee and golden honey and Samson's soft fur. They were a unit, complete within themselves and safe from the isolation of not belonging.

Emily turned away from the window and sat down in the rocking chair, listening to the soothing rise and fall of their voices and the murmur of the sea. *I want to belong, too,* she finally admitted to herself. *God, I want to have a home and family, too.*

A soft but peremptory knock on the door interrupted her solitary reverie.

"Emily?" Simon's voice sounded from the other side. "Let's go for that walk on the beach. There's time before supper."

They strolled around the porch and down a boardwalk that ended at some dunes covered in grass and sea oats. The sand was cool and soft, sifting between Emily's toes and over her ankles as they wandered barefoot down to the deserted beach.

Waves lapped lazily, lifting in slight swells and then sliding onto the smooth shore like a wet, glistening sheet. The setting sun cast a silver sheen over the rippling surface of the waters, and the rest of the world was bathed in the opalescent glow of a September twilight.

"I love to come here," Simon admitted reflectively. "It doesn't seem to matter how majestic the mountains or how serene the woods—there's just something about the rhythm of the sea and the canopy of the sky that draws me closer to God."

He drew Emily's hand through his arm and hugged it to his side. "There's a verse—I think in Psalms—that talks about God wrapping Himself in light. That's what this scene reminds me of."

"It *is* peaceful." She closed her eyes, swallowing against the hard lump rising in her throat.

Simon paused, lifting his hands to cup her face and study it, patterns of green light shifting through his eyes like the waters of the sea. "Emily, share your pain with me. I want to help—please don't shut me out."

Emily tried to back away but was helpless against the strength of those gentle hands, the power of those eyes. Her feet sank into the damp sand as her heart sank into the shifting sands of Simon's moods. He was in turn tender and sensitive, tough and obdurate, wildly passionate. And running through it all, like the sunlight invading the surface of the water, was his abiding faith in God.

How could she fight against something her soul yearned for so deeply, something she found as impossible to believe in as the pot of gold at the end of the rainbow?

"Why do you have so much faith in God?" she blurted out, searching his face with haunted eyes.

Simon's fingers began caressing the shadowed hollows and soft curves of her face. "Because He loves me," he replied simply. "Loved me so much He was willing to sacrifice His only Son. He loves you just as much, Emily Believe that."

"I know." She swallowed, trying to ignore the absent stroking of his fingers. "But it's hard to understand how someone like...well, like *me* rates anything beyond salvation. I'm not important. The world wouldn't come to an end if I did—and God has so many more important things to take care of than to be bothered with my small problems." She put her hands up and pried his away, moving back a few steps. "Besides, if He really cared about me," she said in a moment of honest revelation, "I wouldn't be having all the problems I do."

"Is that how you see God?" Simon questioned casually, without any hint of censure. "As the benign big genie in the sky doling out favors to His children to prove He loves them?"

"Of course not!" Emily flung back, stung in spite of his non-threatening tone.

"Is that what your parents did for you?" he continued, still in the same gentle cadence that nonetheless trampled her abraded feelings like the hooves of a galloping horse. "Gave you all the things you needed—but never gave themselves?"

He saw too much. Somehow he knew too much. Maybe he'd picked Barb's and Taylor's brains. Emily turned on her heel and fled, walking down the beach and leaving a trail of damp footprints behind. How dare he pick and probe her psyche! With each word, he undermined the girders she had so painfully dragged into place over the years to protect herself. And in another minute, he'd have her bawling all over him like a whining baby.

She stepped on a broken shell and staggered, almost falling from the sudden pain. Glancing back, she saw Simon following her, but without any pretense of haste or pursuit. It was as if he knew she had no place to go.

Stunned by the raw finality of that thought, Emily sank down in the sand, heedless of the grittiness and dampness. She couldn't escape from him. She couldn't escape from the person she became when she was around him. She ceased to be the detached, easygoing creature whose feelings were buried so deeply no one ever guessed at the depths or intensity. Instead she became hypersensitive, vulnerable—and ridiculously easy to provoke.

Simon sat down beside her. She could feel his eyes moving over her, but she kept looking out at the water, struggling to withdraw into herself and become as insignificant and unnoticeable as a shell fragment. "Remember the other night when I was pushing you in the swing?" he asked, the question so unexpected Emily's head swiveled toward him, her braid swishing across her back and flipping over her shoulder.

"Yes. Why?"

"We were talking about sunsets then, too." He smiled, a slow smile with the warmth of a golden sunset reflected in it. "Like I said, there's something about being out here that brings me closer to God, and I want you to feel it, too." He relaxed back on his elbows, lifting sand and letting it drift through his fingers. "I believe I mentioned something about how the beauty and inevitability of sunrises and sunsets reminded me of the faithfulness of God."

Emily watched her toes, caked with sand, digging into its coolness as if to hide. "So?" she muttered.

"You never read the verse I asked you to read, did you?" Simon countered without heat. "If you had, you'd understand the point I'm trying to make."

"And what point is that?" Her determined show of indifference was a mistake. With a fluid swiftness so abrupt she didn't have time to react, Simon reared up and grabbed her shoulders, pinning her with his eyes. "No more," he blazed. "I won't let you withdraw anymore, Emily." He leaned forward, his breath fanning her cheek, and the words had no place to go but straight to her heart.

"You've been keeping God at a distance because you're so afraid. You're afraid He doesn't care enough about you to risk trusting Him, just the way you're afraid of me. You bottle up your emotions and give the world the tame, placid version of Emily Carson, and I won't let you get away with it anymore."

"Simon—"

"Well, I'm only a man, and some day I will let you down, or unintentionally hurt you, or fail you because I'm a fallible human being. But God won't ever do that—He can't. It's not possible. Your problem is you just won't accept God's love for you—personally. And it's robbed you of all the confidence and peace to which you're entitled. It's robbed you of joy."

"I don't—"

"You might restore that house and *think* you're happy, satisfied, and secure, but it's a lie. Until you let God restore the joy of your salvation, you'll stay as empty and feel as abandoned as that old place was for fifty years." He leaned closer, and in the rapidly approaching night, his eyes seemed to burn with a fire so bright the sea and sky and sand receded into a single swirl of darkening shadows.

"You've got to open up and allow yourself to believe in that faithfulness because it's as real, as inevitable, as wondrous as the sunset. He's not the one trying to take your house away, or burn it down, or destroy innocent animals, honey. That's all man's doing. God is there, hand stretched out, just waiting for you to take it so He can carry you through."

He released her abruptly and sat back. Then, with a significance that took Emily a moment to grasp, he slowly held out his hand.

Emily sat in the sand, motionless, though her insides were as unstable as a vial of nitroglycerin. Simon was telling her something so significant, so life-changing, that she simply couldn't grasp it. And with his own outstretched hand, he was creating a vivid picture to illustrate the words he had just spoken. What would happen if she put her hand in his? Beyond that, if she symbolically put her hand in the Lord's as Simon wanted her to do?

And what would she do when Simon inevitably let her down, as he had warned her he would?

The silence between them stretched taut, shimmering like a hovering knife blade between Simon's hand and Emily.

She knew that if she refused this outstretched hand, her relationship with Simon—however uncertain it was right now—would be irrevocably altered. Like footprints washed away by a relentless tide, so their relationship would be washed away, the only thing left an impersonal, smooth expanse of beach as untouched, unmarked as before.

Emily had tried to convince herself that she was satisfied with being alone. She had created her world and populated it with people and activities to keep her busy. She had been a comfortable Christian, content to sing in the choir on Sunday mornings and praise the Lord for His goodness. At Easter she had even sung a duet from Handel's "Messiah" proclaiming that He would feed His flock like a shepherd. She had thought she believed it.

She realized now that her faith wasn't the size of a mustard seed. It wasn't even as large as one of these minuscule grains of sand. She also realized that the world she had created for herself would never satisfy her again.

Slowly, heart pounding, Emily lifted her arm and held out her hand. Her fingers trembled.

Hard, warm fingers closed around hers and drew her to her feet. Unnoticed, the last glimmer of sunlight slid into the ocean, and the deep blue sky darkened to the dusky purple a shade away from black. "For a minute," Simon breathed as he drew her into his arms, "I was really afraid." His head descended and his lips brushed the delicate lobe of her ear. "Ah...Emily. Shy and wary—my stubborn sparrow struggling so hard to build her nest...what am I going to do about you?"

"Hal-loo down there, you two!" Nat's voice caught on a sudden breeze and swirled down to them, breaking the mood instantly. "Dinner's on! Come and get it!"

Simon's arms tightened around Emily momentarily, then she was free. "It's just as well," he murmured as they brushed sand off their clothes and then picked their way across the drifting sand to the boardwalk. "Much more time out here with you and I might have gotten carried away. And if my dad found out about that, this time I might have to paint all your porches and be grounded forever."

A smile tugged reluctantly at Emily's lips, then withered. "You'll probably be painting them anyway," she reminded him, dullness coating the words.

He took her arm firmly as they began walking back down the boardwalk and up the stairs to the house. "We'll talk about it tomorrow."

Two days rolled by along with the undulating tides. Emily was stuffed morning, noon, and night with every kind of delectable meal Katherine Balfour could devise.

In between she lolled about on the beach or in a huge old rocker on the porch. Nathaniel taught her the rudiments of chess and took her on long walks along the largely deserted beach.

To Emily's consternation and utter bewilderment, Simon left the house the first morning after they arrived. Katherine explained kindly that there had been some sort of emergency at one of his jobs—they had called after Emily had gone to bed and Simon hadn't wanted to disturb her. She was to sleep in, rest, and be as lazy as an old hound dog napping in the sunshine. He hoped to be back within three days.

Emily accepted this development with equanimity. It was awkward, though, feeling as if she had been beached with Simon's parents like a piece of driftwood, but by lunch of the first day their natural warmth and genuine interest in her helped soften the awkwardness. She still couldn't talk too much about herself, or about the house and her abduction, but she did relax enough to fall back into a facsimile of her former serene, mild-tempered persona.

By suppertime the second night, she was calling the Balfours by their first names without any self-consciousness. She was even sharing in their evening devotionals, luxuriating in their naturalness, their faith that was as much a part of their lives as breathing.

And they included her as if she belonged.

Emily woke on the third morning with a smile on her face for the first time in six months. That morning Nat was going to take her surf fishing, and then Katherine was going to show her how to make the famous biscuits all the men in the family raved about. The first evening Simon had scarfed down four and would have buttered up and downed a fifth, but Nat swiped it right as he was reaching for it and ate it himself, his eyes twinkling at Simon like a cat lapping a saucer full of spilled cream.

With a single-mindedness developed from childhood, Emily managed to lay aside all the worries waiting for her in Georgia. She coveted the time spent with these two people who had welcomed her as if she were their own, coveted it with the greedy desperation of a pearl merchant whose oyster bed was going dry. Because, for all she knew, this would be the only time in her life when she would ever truly feel like a member of a family.

At odd moments, thoughts of her own family intruded, marring the brightness of the day as tarnish on fine old pieces of silver. Emily quickly banished them. She had long ago accepted things the way they were and saw no need to dwell on what hadn't been and could never be. But that was no reason to look this particular gift horse in the mouth.

She stretched beneath the covers, then kicked back the sheet in a sudden burst of energy. Nat had told her the earlier they got down there, the better the fishing would be, and Emily didn't want to keep him waiting. She opened the room-darkening shades covering the windows and gasped in dismay.

It was a little past seven, but there was no sun today. A glowering, slate-colored sky brooded over choppy, restless waters. The sea oats on the tops of the dunes waved wildly in response to a whipping wind, and Emily dropped into the rocking chair and plunked her head on the heels of her hands in dejection. So much for a lovely, relaxing day.

"Doesn't look good," Nat confirmed when Emily

dragged out a little while later.

Katherine's normally pleasant face wore a concerned look today as she poured her husband a second cup of coffee. "What's the weather report now?" she asked, since he had just come back from the den where the television was.

"They're still calling it a tropical storm, since it hasn't turned into hurricane force yet, but if and when it does, we better get the boards up. It's stalled off the Keys, and there's no telling which way it will come."

Emily sat down and thanked Katherine for her cup of coffee. "Have you had many bad hurricanes here?" she asked.

"We've been luckier than a lot of folks," Nat answered and smiled comfortingly as he glanced up and caught the worry in Emily's face. "The last really bad one was a couple years ago. We lost a window and the boardwalk, but the house stood."

"Thanks to you." Katherine laid her hands on her husband's shoulders and kissed his cheek. "Over the years some of the other homes have crumbled like matchsticks from the worst hurricanes. But when Nat builds a house, it's for keeps."

Emily watched the love flow between them and felt a queer wrenching in her heart, a plaintive cry echoing in the barren wasteland of her soul. Nobody had ever looked at her like that or offered the almost worshipful support Katherine and Nat gave to each other. Unwillingly her thoughts strayed to Simon, but there was about as much future in daydreaming over him as there was daydreaming about her house. Both of them were slipping out of her grasp, and Emily years ago had given up trying to hold on to will-o-the-wisps.

After breakfast, Nat and Katherine moved to the den to monitor the weather reports. Emily decided to walk down to the beach since it wasn't raining yet. Somehow the bleak uncertainty of the day matched her mood.

Katherine gave her a Windbreaker to wear because the temperature hovered in the sixties and, with the wind swooping about in erratic gusts, Emily would appreciate something to cover her arms. She gave the younger woman a hug as she held the screen door for her.

"Don't wander too far. Things can deteriorate pretty fast in conditions like this." She smiled into Emily's downcast face. "Of course, thanks to the capriciousness of nature, things could also clear up and this could turn into a mild breezy day. You just have to take each moment as it comes and trust in the Lord to see you through regardless."

Emily knew she wasn't just talking about the weather. "I'm trying to believe that," she confessed sadly. "But it's awfully hard right now."

"I know." Her lined face bathed in concern, Katherine leaned suddenly and pressed a kiss to Emily's cheek. "And we do care, Emily. Not just because my son is fond of you, but because you're *you*."

A lump formed in Emily's throat and stuck. "Thank you," she whispered, and fled.

twelve

Emily walked over an hour, head down against the wind, hair hopelessly tangled as it was whipped and tugged about her back and in her face. She didn't care.

Hands stuffed in the pockets of her jeans, she watched her feet scuffing in the sand and walked. There was no one out this morning, not even the elderly couple she and Nat had met and chatted with on previous mornings.

Beside her, the Gulf of Mexico churned, and on the horizon a lumbering trawler plowed through the heaving water like a dinosaur in a pond shrugging aside a spring zephyr. Emily paid neither the Gulf nor the ship the slightest attention.

The storm in her soul already blew at hurricane force, and she was so caught up in its fury, she was unaware that she was no longer alone on the beach. Only when her downcast eyes fell upon an extra pair of sneakers did she lift her startled gaze and bump into Simon's solid chest.

His hands fastened loosely on her forearms to steady her. "Hello, Emily," he greeted her, his face solemn. The wind was having a heyday with his hair, too, whipping it wildly about so the waves tumbled all over his ears, neck, and forehead. In contrast, his mouth remained a straight, unsmiling line.

Emily couldn't help it. She stared up at him, revealing all the confusion and wariness and hopeless longing. Simon groaned deep in his chest, jerked her against him, and kissed her.

"Why did you do that?" Emily gasped out when at last he lifted his mouth and set her a little ways from him.

"Because I wanted to. And don't ask me why, or I'll do it again just to shut you up." He snuggled the two unzipped panels of her Windbreaker beneath her chin, the knuckles of his hands brushing the soft underside of her throat.

"What gives you the right—" Emily sputtered, indignation and alarm kicking through her, but her protest was abruptly silenced as Simon carried out his threat. When he lifted his head this time, Emily was clinging to his neck and shoulders, legs weak as water.

"You are the most baffling, frustrating woman I've ever known." His fingers danced across the surface of her skin, skimming an electrifying message over her windstung face and the little pulse hammering in her throat. "And for some reason I'm attracted to you more strongly than I've ever been to another woman. You, on the other hand, seem to think you're about as desirable as lukewarm cream of wheat."

"It's the truth," she slurred the words.

Simon administered a brief but firm shake. "Stop it!" he demanded, temper whipping through the words like the wind was their hair. "Look at me, Emily!"

She opened her eyes, hands moving to push against his chest in an effort to be free. "What are you trying to do to me?" she wailed, struggling to cope with the extreme shifts of his moods. "You cuddle me up, then tear me down. You kiss me, and then you yell at me. You tell me you find me attractive, and then you treat me like a scummy rag!"

Simon was not fooled by Emily's display of temper. He might have succeeded in riling her enough to momentarily break her out of her misery and depression, but he had also confused and frightened her. That, of course, made him a stupid, insensitive jerk. *Help me, Lord.* If he weren't careful, he could lose the battle altogether, and hence the war.

There was something else he had to tell her, and because he'd been stalling, he had ended up muddying the issue by dragging feelings into it. But when he'd seen her walking out here looking so lost and alone, he couldn't stand it, especially when she looked at him with those huge dark eyes. God knew how desperately he was trying to control his feelings, but it was getting harder. When she found out his news, she probably wouldn't let him any closer than a mile.

"Emily," he allowed with a sigh, "I know I'm a first-class heel, even though all I wanted was to jar you out of your depression. I can't apologize for kissing you, but I will admit to lousy timing." He waited, but when Emily refused to respond, he took a deep breath and took the plunge. "There's something I need to explain, and after you hear what it is, maybe you'll understand why I'm behaving the way I am."

"That's a first class excuse," Emily finally retorted, the words muffled because she had her hands over her face now.

Simon groaned. "Emily, are you crying on me?"

"No! Yes. What if I am? I feel like a yo-yo the way you're acting. It's...humiliating." She faltered, caught her breath on a sob, and tried once more to move around him.

"Emily...please. I'm sorry. Don't go in yet." He waited in agony, his eyes on her bent head and the rigid line of her back. After a long, painful moment, she slowly turned around, but she still wouldn't look at him. Simon allowed his pent-up breath to escape in a long sigh, and with a hesitant gesture of repentance, he reached and brushed his fingers across her cheekbone.

"I'm not providing you with a very loving example of God's faithfulness, am I?" he observed, chagrin coating the words. "Unless you keep in mind that at least I do keep coming back, even if it's only to confuse you more."

Almost, she smiled. She lifted her head and faced him with an expression as blank as a sheet of fresh typing paper. "What else did you want to tell me?"

His eyes flickered briefly, but he didn't sidetrack this time. "I have something to tell you about Aunt Iris, and it isn't very pleasant, though I doubt it will come as a surprise."

"She's suing me." She made the statement matter-of-factly, but Simon knew her better. He opened his mouth, but Emily interrupted. "Why didn't you just tell me, instead of...initiating that...display a few moments ago?"

Simon buried his hands deep in the hip pockets of the chinos he was wearing and gave her a candid answer. "I couldn't help it. You looked so lost and alone, and I was about to make it even worse. I wanted to wipe away that lost look and wake you up to how I really felt. I know I'm coming across irrationally, and I do apologize for it." He dropped his gaze to his feet, then lifted it back to Emily's coffee-dark eyes. "But with God as my witness, I'll never *deliberately* hurt you. Never. Can you try to believe that at least?"

After lunch Simon announced their decision to return to Georgia.

"Emily is going to need to talk with her lawyer, and I'm going to see what's happening with the sleaze balls trespassing on her land." He watched Emily grimly, hating the whole mess with a vehemence bordering on homicidal.

"Wouldn't it be better if she stayed with her friends?" his father commented.

Simon nodded his head at Emily, his expression remote. "You try to convince her. I gave up an hour ago." A muscle in his jaw quivered as he battled his frustration. "For two cents I'd leave her here, but knowing her, she'd simply hike down to the main road and hitch a ride."

Emily smiled across the room at him. "You're just a poor loser," she stated with false sweetness. "It may not be my home much longer, but while it is I plan to live in it. No slimy low-lifes are going to frighten me away, and—"

"The next time they might do more than frighten you," Simon interrupted harshly. "Why do you insist on being so pig-headed, woman?"

"Simon," his mother interjected, doubt and dismay so blatant Emily turned her head away. "How about our tagging along with you? We could stay at Emily's—"

"No!" both Simon and Emily chorused in emphatic agreement.

"We don't need to go providing them with any more ammunition," Simon stated flatly. "I've talked to the sheriff. He promises around-the-clock protection, for a while anyway—as long as he can. But I don't want you two involved. It's bad enough having Emily in the thick of it."

"I can take care of myself."

Simon sliced her an impatient look. "Like you did the day you landed in the hospital?"

Emily slumped in defeat. "I'll go make sure my bag is packed," she mumbled, walking past Simon with downcast head.

His father waited until Emily shut her door, then

motioned for Simon to follow him into the kitchen while Katherine followed Emily. "Don't you think you're being a mite bossy?" he observed mildly, and Simon flushed.

"I can't seem to help it. She won't listen to reason. I know she's hurting, not only over the drug issue, but now this confounded lawsuit." He slammed his hands down on the counter, rattling the dishes drying in the drainer next to him.

"Why did she have to find the will? It's almost impossible to get through to her now. She's clammed up inside herself so tightly and so blindly that she has no idea of what could happen to her all alone in that big old mausoleum." He whirled and faced his father. "I'm beginning to hate the place, you know. Hate it because it's going to cost me the woman I—"

He stopped, stunned, and then groaned aloud, covering his eyes with the back of his hand. "I'm in love with her," he confessed, and dropped his hand to stare across at his father. "If something happens to her—if Aunt Iris takes the place away from her—I don't know if I'll be able to stand it."

Nathaniel laid his arm around his son's shoulders. "I know...I know. You're just going to have to do a lot of praying—and as much protecting as she'll allow." He grinned a little bit. "But if you'll take the suggestion of the old man who reared you and suffered through your wild youth, try honey instead of vinegar. Emily might not be a militant feminist, but she's been on her own too long to fall tamely in line with your commands."

"If I try that approach I doubt I could maintain my Christian code of ethics, Dad," Simon responded dryly. "And Emily's...untouched."

Nathaniel lifted an eyebrow. "That's refreshing—and

a relief from a parental point of view. I thought she looked—I guess 'unawakened' would be the word."

"And you don't know how badly I'd like to awaken her." Simon examined his fingernails, then met his father's smug expression. "That's right—gloat. You and Mom have been trying to marry me off for ten years now."

He contemplated his hands as if wondering whether he'd like to wrap them around Emily to caress her—or throttle her. "I suppose you realize that persuading her to marry me will be about as easy as the Arabs and Jews negotiating a truce in Jerusalem."

"I trust you'll control yourself, son, and remember your Christian convictions, regardless of your feelings."

"I'm not going to seduce her, Dad, if that's what you're getting at." Simon straightened, giving his father the sort of stark honesty he had given him all his life. "I do want to make love to her, because I love her—even if I only acknowledged it this moment. But it's because I *do* love and desire her so much that I can wait. Do you have any idea what it means to me to know that if she'll marry me, I'll be the first—and only?"

"I know. I pray God will grant you the chance, if Emily is truly the woman He has picked out to be your mate." He cleared his throat, and his eyes were damp. "She's a pretty special lady. Your mother and I would love to have her as a daughter."

"Thanks, Dad." Simon squared his shoulders and moved toward the hall. "I better see what's keeping her and Mom. There's no telling what Emily may try. Being around her is like trying to catch hold of fog."

"Knowing your mother, she just might succeed. And then present your elusive lady to you for Christmas."

thirteen

The nearer they came to the Georgia border, the more nervous Emily felt. Simon was strangely pensive and even more strangely non-aggressive. He hadn't tried to talk her out of going to the house anymore, and he hadn't badgered her about how to handle the lawsuit and what she ought to say to Brad. If she hadn't been so worried about the future, Emily would have been hurt.

As it was, she found herself wishing Simon would at least talk to her, even if it was only about the weather, which was gray and drizzling and miserable. When she was looking out the window, all her mind did was scrabble frantically around the problems she faced, without offering any solutions. "Simon?" she finally asked, almost whispering.

"Hmm?"

"If I admit I'm a little bit scared, will you jump down my throat and say `I told you so'?"

His hands tightened on the steering wheel, and he shot her a brief look that encompassed a galaxy of emotions. "Have I been that terrible, Emily?"

She puzzled at the hint of hurt, the nuance of despair. "You haven't always been sweet and understanding."

He scowled at that. "What do you expect when you insist on modeling yourself after a sitting duck?"

"Nothing, I suppose." She choked down the hurt and resumed contemplating the countryside.

A few minutes later Simon pulled off into a deserted

roadside picnic area. A misting rain slid down the windshield, blurring the surroundings now that the wipers were no longer swishing back and forth. The atmosphere inside the car thickened until Simon commanded very quietly, "Come here, Emily," and pointed to the space beside him.

"Why?" Emily responded warily, her body stiffening with suspicion and a strange sort of excitement.

"Because I've decided to try my hand at being sweet and understanding for a change. Now come here."

"I didn't mean to hurt your feelings," Emily grumbled, but she undid her seat belt and slid over.

"That's better," he murmured huskily. "Now...put your arms around me and kiss me."

"What? What's that supposed to prove?" She floundered about, looking everywhere but at Simon.

He uttered a low laugh, picked up the end of her braid, and began winding it around his fist until she was forced to move right against him, their faces inches apart. "No problem," he breathed. "I don't mind kissing you...."

His mouth closed over hers, kissing her with tender thoroughness and consummate skill. Emily's arms crept up over his shoulders and clung to him as she gave herself up to the incandescent cloud of feelings. She could feel Simon's heartbeat thundering, its wild cadence matching hers, and she marveled that she really did seem to affect him so strongly.

After awhile his hands released her and gently removed her arms from around his neck. "Now, relax and let me give you the reassurance you're so desperate for."

He held her head against his chest and stroked her hair, all the passion wiped away as if it had never been. "I'm trying, you see," he murmured above her head, "to teach you that you *can* trust me, at least physically."

Emily gradually relaxed, and at last closed her eyes with a low murmur of contentment. If only he would be like this all the time. If only she *could* trust him. She stirred restlessly, and his arms tightened.

"Be still," he coaxed. "Be still and rest, sparrow-girl. It's going to be all right. Everything is going to be all right. Because regardless of how things turn out, regardless of how you feel about me—God will be there, taking care of you." He paused, then added in such low tones that Emily wasn't sure she heard, "And so will I."

The next morning when Emily called Brad to tell him she'd be in to resume her secretarial duties, he did not try to hide his relief. He did tell her that they would also take the time to have a lawyer-to-client chat, but she was not to worry about a thing.

Emily wondered if Simon would fuss about her going back to work so soon, but he smoothly agreed with her decision, pointing out that she would be a lot safer thirty miles away in Sylvan anyway. Emily sourly reminded him that she was not a two year old who needed coddling and then clamped her mouth shut. She was feeling raw after a crying jag the night before. Somewhere inside her lived a two year old whose feelings were bruised because Simon had made no effort to console or coddle her.

She drove the miles to Sylvan in uneasy silence. It was really no wonder Simon acted so unpredictably around her. She pushed him away with one arm and clung with the other. Heat stole into her cheeks as she relived her unbridled response in the car coming back from Florida.

Simon must think her a totally desperate woman willing to take any crumbs he cared to toss her way—and if the price was patting her shoulder and telling her things would be all right...well, he *had* come through with his end of the bargain.

It was no use. She was mooning and pining over him like the girls in her eighth grade classes pined over a high school junior. The only difference was that the girls had a better chance of landing a date with the junior than Emily did landing Simon Balfour. In spite of everything he kept telling her, he was still out of her league. Way out.

"Things are never that bad." Brad greeted her glum countenance with a cheery welcome smile that didn't try to hide his open relief. "Here. Have a stick of strawberry gum—a gal I met in Albany gave me a couple of packs."

"No thanks." She tried to produce an answering smile as she put her purse under the desk, but it wavered. "Brad, I'm scared."

Brad's cheerfulness disappeared behind his bland lawyer's mask. "Let's just take things one at a time, all right? You worry about secretarying and let me worry about the legal matters."

That, unfortunately, was easier said than done, as Emily found out when she was sitting across from him later that afternoon. Brad did not try to confuse her by spouting off legal terminology, but he did not mince words either.

"As I warned you, Ms. Bancroft has filed in probate court to prove the validity of the will I gather it was your dubious honor to find." He chewed a few moments on his third stick of the strawberry gum, drumming his fingers on his desk. "It was in a safety deposit box hidden behind the closet wall in your bedroom, Lamar told me."

Emily nodded. Her own hands were clenched tightly between her knees, and despite the pleasant coolness of the day, she could feel perspiration dotting her brow and dampening her palms. "Simon dropped it off at Mr. Hansell's office on our way to Florida. He figured the sooner we got it over with, the better."

"Hmm," Brad replied unhelpfully. "Well, they certainly didn't let any grass grow under their feet, which I suppose isn't surprising after meeting Ms. Bancroft." He gave a reluctant grin. "Formidable woman, isn't she?"

"I don't stand a chance," Emily declared miserably.

"Now, now, don't insult your lawyer," Brad chided, but he didn't disagree with her. "I've got about three weeks to dig up some other court decisions that will support our position. You concentrate on being my secretary and keeping yourself safe." He looked across at her. "Are you staying with Barb and Taylor?"

"N...no." She couldn't sustain the alert look of suspicion that entered his face, and dropped her gaze. "I'm staying at the house. Sheriff Jessup has assigned two men to guard the place, and I know the DEA is also—"

"Emily, that's insane!" Brad jackknifed up out of his chair, raking his fingers through the thick thatch of blond hair. "Where is your Sir Galahad, anyway? Or has he kissed you off now that the will has been found?"

Emily found herself unaccountably angry at the disparaging reference to Simon, and caution was thrown to the winds. "He most certainly has *not* 'kissed me off!' In fact, he's promised that as long as I live in the house, he won't leave until the men who abducted me are behind bars." The words resounded off the filing cabinets and hovered in the air like a burst of fireworks on the Fourth of July. Emily watched with dismay the incredulity and disillusionment wash over Brad's lean, attractive face.

"Not only does that make you a sitting duck for another abduction, or worse, but under the present circumstances, Balfour's presence could be construed as even more of a conflict of interest than your working for me."

"I don't know why the two of you insist on behaving like snapping turtles," Emily muttered, exasperated. "The main reason he's staying is because he's doing most of the restoration work now—and yes, it's because I gave him permission."

Brad sat back down and casually propped his feet on the desk, crumpling several papers in the process. "Snapping turtles, huh?" He contemplated the ceiling with a bland expression Emily hated. "Are you telling me Balfour has been suggesting libelous interpretations of my actions toward you—with no evidence to substantiate his claims, I might add?"

"Quit talking like a lawyer!" Emily retorted.

Brad burst into laughter. "Boy, have you got it bad! Do you leap as hotly to my defense with Balfour?"

Emily gave a disdainful sniff. "I have better things to do than sit around while you mock me. If our—consultation—is finished, I'm leaving. I need to go by the grocery store."

For a laid-back lawyer, Brad could move with startling speed, blocking the door before Emily had taken more than two steps. "Come down off your high horse, Emily. I was only teasing you, and you know it."

"Sounded more like harassment to me."

Brad folded his arms across his chest. "Stop talking like a lawyer," he mimicked.

Giving up, Emily finally laughed. She returned to retrieve her purse, aware that Brad was still watching her even as he stepped aside. Emily did not trust the look on his face at all—it reminded her of Simon. "See you day after tomorrow," she tossed out lightly.

"Okey-dokey." Just before she reached the bottom stair he called to her. "Emily?"

She twisted her head around. "What?"

"Be careful with Balfour, will you? I don't trust him."

Emily's face closed up like elevator doors. "Neither," she enunciated carefully, "do I."

fourteen

The court date was set for the first week in November. Emily told Simon, and he watched her carefully circle the date on her wall calendar hanging in the kitchen.

Autumn arrived and the last of summer withered with the last of the honeysuckle and wisterias. Some of the bronze mums Emily had planted back in July bloomed, and Simon helped arrange them in a jar on the kitchen table. The monthly missive from Emily's parents showed a dramatic New England fall, and Emily taped it on the wall above the mums. Simon tactfully made no comment.

He spent most days working on a different area of the house from Emily, though any time she asked for help, he willingly obliged. Most of his evenings were spent in his portable office.

One week he'd had to spend in Tennessee, tying up work on the eighty-year old stone cottage. The two deputies had been re-assigned due to lack of funds and staff, but Sheriff Jessup arranged their return while Simon was gone. Emily, quieter with each passing week, barely protested. Without telling her, after returning from Tennessee, Simon re-negotiated the dates for his next job, postponing work until after Christmas.

Two days before the hearing, he was on the side veranda, applying a wood preservative to the yellow pine floorboards he had replaced. He was enjoying himself so much that it was almost easy to forget the reason he was able to do the work in the first place. Everett VanCleef certainly had built this place to last, for there was surprisingly little deterioration even though the house had been unattended for almost fifty years.

Simon had repaired mortar joints in the bricks, and with Emily's permission had hired a local carpenter to help replace a sill and several of the joists under the porches which had succumbed to rot. But other than three windowsills on the north and east side of the house that had also needed replacing, the exterior wood structures were fairly sound. Yep, Everett sure had wanted this house to last, and considering the terms of his feudal will, it shouldn't have been too surprising.

The will.

The hearing, now only two days away.

Simon plopped the brush down and sat back on his heels a minute, tension curling his spine. That blasted will!

Every time Simon caught Emily in the library, gazing at the leaded glass window with agony in her eyes, it took every ounce of self-control to keep from cleaning the window himself, then falling at Emily's feet and confessing his love. More than anything on this earth, Simon wished for providential blessing to restore both woman and window to their light and beauty.

If I keep a lid on my temper and try extra hard to wait on You, Lord, is there a chance? And no, I'm not trying to bargain. I just can't help wanting to know, wanting—

"Simon..."

He jerked out of his prayerful reverie with a start, lifting his head to where Emily was standing just outside the french doors leading onto the veranda. In one swift, encompassing glance, he marked the colorless complexion and the way she was clutching the front of her sweatshirt with her hand. His eyes zeroed in on the hand, which was covered in blood.

He was by her side in two swift strides. "What happened?"

"I was trying to replace that broken pane—the one you picked up at the store yesterday for me...." She gasped a little as Simon gently pried loose her hand and exposed the wound.

"Easy, love." It was a nasty cut, a diagonal slash across the back of her wrist, and it was bleeding heavily. "Here—hold it up—that's it...." He whipped his handkerchief out and placed it directly on the cut, applying a firm steady pressure and talking to her in a low, soothing voice. "It's okay, Emily. It's okay. Come on, now, and let's get you to the bathroom and clean you up. At least it's the back of your wrist instead of the front." He gave her what he hoped was an encouraging smile. "You could have been a first class klutz and gone for the artery."

"You're so reassuring," Emily muttered faintly. "I'm bleeding to death and all you do is make disparaging remarks about my abilities." For some reason—probably because she was tired and worried and still insecure—she took offense at his teasing remark instead of responding in kind.

After sitting her down, Simon lifted her chin with his free hand. "I wasn't denigrating your work," he promised softly. "You've done a great job, and I'm proud of you."

Her head lifted. "You are?"

Simon gazed down into her incredulous, suddenly smiling eyes. *Lord, I love this woman.* His fingers stroked a tender path across her soft lips. "Yes," he affirmed deeply, "I am. Now take a deep breath and lean on me. This is going to sting."

He wouldn't allow her to work any more that day, bullying her into sitting on the veranda in a deck chair Barb had donated so she could watch him work. Emily submitted both to his doctoring and gentle dictatoring with such a hazy, dreamy acquiescence Simon wanted to shout aloud his feelings. She *was* softening, responding to him now. Soon, very soon he would confess his love, and pray she would reciprocate. *I can't wait much longer, Lord.* He refused to speculate about the aftermath of the hearing.

They whiled away the afternoon in rich harmony, with Simon savoring every moment. As he worked, he shared stories of various homes he had restored and the sometimes hair-raising tales of the owners he'd had to contend with. Emily countered with similar hair-raising stories of her life as a junior high teacher, relaxing into the serene, warm, and compassionate woman she was when she wasn't feeling threatened.

Early Wednesday morning, Simon drove Emily to Sylvan to spend the day and night with Barb and Taylor, while he flew to pick up Iris. Emily had withdrawn again, treating him to the remote, polite facade she'd perfected since the trip to Florida. Simon hung onto his temper, but it was an effort. The thirty-mile trip seemed twice that long because of the grim silence that hung between them. Finally they reached Barb and Taylor's home.

"Heard any developments on the drug ring?" Taylor asked in a low voice while Barb dithered over Emily's bandaged wrist.

Simon shook his head. "Last week a plane was sighted taking off from a field two counties west of here, and a Customs agent managed to track it until bad weather closed in and they lost it. Nothing else has turned up so far, and we don't know if it's the same people or not."

He didn't tell Taylor (who would tell Barb) that a weekly check by Sheriff Jessup of the woods surrounding Emily's property had turned up evidence of a recently used campsite. That in itself was ominous but inconclusive, so Simon had chosen not to burden Emily or her friends with the information.

She wouldn't appreciate his decision, he knew. Abruptly, Simon wanted to pound his fist through a wall. He interrupted Barb by stepping in front of her and turning to Emily. "Walk me back to the car?" He cupped her elbow and smiled at Barb.

"Trying to flaunt your power?" Emily observed snidely once they were outside, and Simon counted to twenty.

"I know you're feeling pretty defensive and vulnerable right now," he returned, very quietly, "but I wish you'd try trusting me for a change instead of automatically assuming the worst."

Emily flicked him one look of shattering pain. "I can't trust you. I won't." Her chin jutted. "And if your great-aunt wins tomorrow I'll pack my bags and you won't see me for the dust."

The chill of her pronouncement rang in Simon's ears long after he drove off, and he knew the look on her face would haunt him the rest of his life.

Taylor took the day off so he could drive with Emily and Barb to Timmons. It was a muggy day, so hot and close the crispness of autumn might have been a dream. In the deep south, summer and fall often waged a contest throughout November, with the dreary dripping rains of winter finally ending the battle.

Barb had taken Emily in hand, forcing her to choke down half a grapefruit and a slice of cheese toast for breakfast and then picking out what she should wear to the hearing. Emily had brought along the brown suit and cream blouse she'd worn the first time, but Barb regarded the outfit with disdain.

"You don't need to look like you're going to prison, and that's about what all those neutral shades do for you." She began plundering her closet, muttering imprecations since her dress size was at least two sizes larger than Emily's. "Haven't you listened to anything I've tried to tell you over the last couple years about your needing to wear brighter colors?"

"I'm not auditioning for a beauty contest, Barb." Emily sat listlessly on the edge of the bed, brushing out her hair with halfhearted strokes. Her bandaged wrist made this awkward, and the cut throbbed a little. "I frankly don't care how I look."

Barb ignored her. "Here—try this blouse. You'll have to wear the suit, but we can at least liven it up a little. With the jacket on and the way this blouse is supposed to drape in folds, no one will notice that it's a little big."

Emily eyed the brightly patterned blouse swirling in vivid shades of burnt orange, red, and sienna. When she put it on with her brown suit, the difference was startling. Emily glanced in the mirror and shrugged. "It's okay, I suppose. Thanks, Barb."

She sat in the back seat as they drove to Timmons, ignoring the glances Barb kept casting over the seat and the looks Taylor sneaked in the rearview mirror. She was clammy and cold in spite of the sultry day, and wondered if she would ever be warm again. Brad had tried to reassure her yesterday before she left the office, but he was not hopeful and was too good a lawyer to lie. Emily could feel the shroud of hopelessness bearing her down, down into a cold pit of nothingness.

All her life she had wondered why she wasn't loved, what lack in her existed that kept her parents from loving her enough to provide her with the love and security her soul needed and craved. J.J. had fought his way to recognition, but all it had earned him in the end was trouble until he grasped the life ring of the Air Force Emily had tossed to him so desperately. He had never bothered to toss her anything in return, and Emily had learned to go her own way because no one would ever care enough to help her out.

And now, just when she had finally found something to call her own, something that needed to be needed—just like herself—it was going to be yanked away from her. *God,* she found herself praying, *God, what am I going to do? What's the matter with me? This is even worse than being held upside down in a bag, not knowing if I was going to live or die. I don't have a choice now—I have to keep on living, but Lord, I feel dead inside.*

"When hope within me dies...I draw over closer to Him...." The single line of melody whispered across her heartstrings, so faint and haunting that for a moment she actually caught her breath, straining to hear. "From care He sets me free...." The music was stronger now, and the words plucked a little louder, sounding in her head like chimes. "His eye is on the sparrow... and I know He watches me—His eye is on the sparrow, and I know He watches me."

The song. Simon had told her she reminded him of that

song—that's why to this day he sometimes called her sparrow-girl. It aggravated her, infuriated her, irritated her—but not until this moment did she feel the comfort and reassurance the nickname also offered. Emily had only been concentrating on the unflattering ramifications of being a sparrow—plain, brown, and not worth looking at twice.

Simon had tried to tell her differently, but she hadn't listened. She closed her eyes, bowing her head to force out all the other intrusive sounds. She wanted to listen now. She pictured the battered hymnbook Mrs. Jenkins had given her and tried to focus on the page on which the song was printed. There was something about being afraid, about clouds. Why had she just stuffed the book in a box of other forgotten paraphernalia when she moved out of the apartment? The words were hovering on the tip of her tongue, so close she could—

That was it! "...draw over closer to Him...From care He sets me free...." *Lord, I would give anything—including that house, if I could draw closer to You and know You cared about me. Simon claims You do, and he certainly acts like he's got an inside track to Your ear, but then he's been a lot more faithful to You over the years than I have.*

The haunting melody deepened into the baritone chords of Simon's voice reciting another Bible verse. What was it? Something about salvation, restoring the joy....

"Emily? You okay? We're almost there." Barb's voice intruded suddenly, shattering the melody Emily was straining to hear.

Emily lifted her head and forced a smile. "I'm okay, Barb. Believe it or not, I was actually praying."

Barb looked abashed. "I'm sorry, Emily." She reached a hand over the seat to Emily, and after a brief hesitation Emily's lifted in response. "Everyone has been praying for you, even the kids." She squeezed Emily's hand, then let it go as Taylor slowed to pull into the diagonal parking space in front of the stately, columned courthouse.

They were a little late, and when the three of them walked inside the same drab waiting room as before, it was already crowded with people. Their case was not the first one on the docket this morning, and there were a half dozen or so other equally nervous individuals all waiting their turn.

Everyone else blurred in Emily's eyes when she caught sight of Simon. For the past three months, they had lived like friendly next door neighbors who worked together, and for most of that time Emily succeeded in regarding Simon in that light.

Now—with a single glance—everything had changed. He was sitting beside Iris, looking so solid and capable and masculine next to Iris's petite fragility that Emily's mouth went powder dry. He was wearing a charcoal pinstripe suit with a mint green silk shirt and coordinating tie, the effect lending him an aura of leashed power and raw elegance Emily had never really noticed. The thick waves of his rich, nutmeg-brown hair radiated health and vitality, and the same sizzling life leaped out of his eyes when he saw Emily.

Something sizzled in Iris Bancroft's gray eyes as well, but it was the cold sizzling of steam rising off frozen steel, and it was also frankly triumphant. Her snappy cardinal red suit, tailored gray blouse, and matching gloves made Emily feel like a frumpy dowager instead of the other way around.

Simon started across to meet her immediately. Brad,

talking in the corner with Lamar Hansell, also caught sight of her. He excused himself, a grim, determined look behind his deceptively lazy, charming demeanor.

"How are you doing? Did you sleep at all?" Simon was asking her in a husky undertone, his gaze moving over her face, her hair, dropping to the suit and Barb's blouse. "That's a pretty blouse—lots better than the one you wore the last time."

Emily bit her lip to keep from smiling. He was trying so hard. "It's Barb's. You'll have to tell her you approve of her taste better than mine."

"Emily." Brad was at her elbow. "We need to discuss a few things."

For a spine-tingling moment the air froze into an aura rife with unspoken threats and warnings. Emily glanced from Brad to Simon, trying to comprehend why the hairs on the back of her neck were tingling, and why Simon looked, well, almost primitive, as if he were about to rip Brad apart like a ravaging wolf devouring a piece of raw meat.

Feeling uneasy, uncertain, she shifted her gaze over Simon's shoulder and met head-on the frozen glare of Iris Bancroft. But there was an arrested gleam there as well, an almost reluctant dawning of awareness Emily didn't understand any more than she did Simon's behavior.

Then the moment passed as Brad tugged her away and Taylor moved up beside Simon, asking him a question and forcing the younger man's attention.

"Brr," Brad shivered as he led Emily over to the only two vacant chairs left in the room. "Your watchdog is growling awfully noisily for someone who only wants to restore your house, Ms. Carson. He almost acts jealous, if you ask me."

"I thought you had something you needed to talk to me about," Emily reminded him, faint color staining her bleached out cheeks.

Brad smiled a little, but took the hint. He dropped down in the chair beside her, glanced off to the left, then deliberately lifted Emily's hand and held it comfortingly between his own. "Emily, you know this doesn't look good, but I wanted to remind you that we still have the option of filing a counter suit ourselves if the judge decides in the plaintiff's favor this time."

Emily shook her head. "I can't take any more, Brad." She looked up at him hopelessly. "I know you've done the best you could—probably better than any other lawyer could have done—but if this goes the way I think it will, I'm throwing in the towel." She swallowed, then finished in a tone so low Brad barely heard, "Simon will do a better job on the house with me gone, anyway."

Brad cursed softly but succinctly, then issued a gruff apology when Emily winced. She found herself noting with stunning irrelevance that Simon had never once used foul language or curse words in her presence. He liked ordering her about, lost his temper with her—even yelled at her, but never had he blasphemed or employed gutter language to vent his anger and frustration. He wasn't perfect and was honest enough to admit it, but Simon Balfour was a committed Christian to the core. She might not ever be able to trust him—but she *did* trust his faith.

"Emily!" Brad was jiggling her hand, and she looked at him, eyes wide and startled. "It's time to go. They're calling our case."

He kept her hand tucked in his elbow as they all moved toward the door. Simon shot Brad a murderous glare and Brad merely deflected it with a provocative grin, but dread had reared up and grabbed Emily's throat and she didn't notice anything.

She remained a motionless statue as the court was brought to order and the case presented. The judge retired once again to his chambers. No emotion ruffled the barren desert of her countenance when, as predicted, the judge returned to set aside his prior decision, determining that the validity of the will should prevail over Emily's later title.

Voices gusted around her like breezes, but she sat unmoving, feeling as if layers of clear polyurethane were being applied around and around her. She was present, but unreachable. Barb's arm was around her, and Taylor was patting her shoulder. Brad said something, but he was talking with Mr. Hansell now and whatever he told her slid right off.

He came back a minute later and took her hand. "Listen, Em, I know what a blow this is. Why don't you hang up secretarying for me awhile and try to just rest—get your perspective back. Gloria will be able to come back in a week anyway, and I can manage until then." The voices around Emily rose suddenly, as if someone were arguing, and a warm, strong hand on her arm was urging her to rise.

"—just leave her alone!" Barb was snarling. "Go gloat with your old biddy of a great-aunt!"

"I don't think you understand." The hand tightened, and Emily found herself standing. "I'm not asking your permission."

She was being led down the short aisle and out of the courtroom, and because it was Simon, her senses swam into a sharp stabbing moment of focus. "Please leave me alone," she stated clearly.

"Not on your life."

"Wait a minute, Balfour!" That was Brad's voice coming closer again. "I need to—"

Simon halted, jerking around with Emily following like a boneless rag doll. "You don't need to do anything but back off," Simon suggested so quietly, so deliberately, that Brad did just that. "Whatever formalities need to be handled you can either handle yourself or wait. I'm taking Emily someplace private, and I'm taking her now."

Emily wanted to summon up the energy to fling aside his hand and unleash the temper she had discovered she had after she met Simon. It stayed locked up somewhere in the frozen storage area of her heart, though, and she ended up allowing herself to be hustled out of the courthouse, down the steps, and into Simon's Jensen-Healy without even lifting her little pinkie.

"What about your great-aunt?" she inquired with polite detachment.

"Lamar is taking her to his home. We'll pick her up later." He drove several blocks to a small park and playground, parked, got out, and came around and helped Emily out. Keeping her hand firmly in his, he walked her over to a wooden park bench placed between two towering pines.

He sat her down, then joined her, turning so he could watch her, his hands reaching out to grip her shoulders. "Emily," he sighed her name almost as if in prayer. "Emily, you don't have to lose the house. You don't even have to leave it." He shook her gently, forcing her eyes to focus on him so he knew she was taking in his words. "Emily—sparrow-girl—I want you to marry me."

fifteen

Emily was staring at him blankly. "You want me to marry you?" she parroted in a dull monotone. "Why? The house belongs to your great-aunt now. You can restore it however you like. Why marry *me*?"

"Because I'm in love with you!" he all but snapped. "Why else would I ask you to marry me?" His hands slid down her arms, back up to cup her face. "Did you hear me? I love you."

For a brief instant something stirred inside her, as if a flickering spark buried deep under the ashes was struggling to re-ignite. Then she shook her head, lifting her own hands to gently but firmly remove his. "You don't love me—you just feel sorry for me." She forced a painful smile. "It's okay, Simon. I'll be okay after awhile, but I appreciate the gesture."

She made as if to rise, then a startled gasp escaped her restricted throat when Simon jerked her completely off her feet and into his lap. He wrapped her in a firm embrace, his face thrust inches away from hers.

"I do not feel sorry for you, woman!" he growled. "I said I love you, and that is *exactly* what I meant. I've never told a woman that before, and I hadn't planned on telling you yet. But now that I have, you better believe it, or we'll have the first shotgun wedding in America where the bride*groom's* father is holding the shotgun instead of the bride's!"

"Nobody loves me like that," Emily whispered. "They

never have—why should you?"

He groaned, and began covering her face with kisses. "You are loved, Emily Carson," he promised fervently, feverishly. "You are lovable, and you are loved. By me, by all your friends—by your heavenly Father." His mouth found hers, and he kissed her long and deeply. "Marry me, Emily. Marry me, and we'll restore the house and our lives together."

"No." She began shaking her head, and couldn't seem to stop. "No. You don't really love me, and I won't trap us both. Leave me alone, Simon, please. Take me back and leave me alone." When his arms merely tightened, she began to struggle, but the efforts were weak, sluggish, as if all her batteries had run completely down. "Let me go," she whimpered, perilously close to breaking.

Simon released her, watching with tortured gaze as she scrambled up and backed away, hands shaking as she straightened her rumpled suit and hair. His hand lifted, reaching out, pleading. "Emily—please try to believe me. I love you. As God is my witness, I love you as much as a man can love a woman. Love, Emily. Not pity."

The tears began then, a slow, hot trickle that slipped over the pooling rims and slid down her ashen cheeks. "I wish I could believe you," she sighed in a choked undertone. "I've always wished I could believe you." Lifeless, defeated, she stood in front of him, inches away, the tears falling unheeded. She might as well have been on another planet.

"We'll discuss it later." He took out a handkerchief and wiped his face, looking exhausted—but determined. "Let's go fetch Aunt Iris."

"I'd rather not. She won't want to be anywhere near me."

"You leave Aunt Iris to me."

"I suppose you expect to be tossed out on your ear," Iris Bancroft announced in a reedy patrician voice, setting down her glass of iced tea and fixing Emily with a penetrating gaze. "You certainly look like you're facing a firing squad."

"Aunt Iris—"

"Stay out of this, boy. You've caused me enough trouble in the last months to put me on digitalis." Her ivory-handled cane thumped on the Oriental rug of Lamar Hansell's study. "I heartily disapprove of your actions, but of course you're aware of that, I dare say."

"You've made it pretty clear," Simon returned calmly. "But what you don't seem to understand is that I love Emily, and I'm going to marry her."

Iris surveyed him archly, the merest suggestion of a smile softening the severity of her lined, narrow face. "I understand quite well," she refuted, and emitted a disdainful sniff. "Just because I never married myself doesn't make me blind, deaf, and dumb. You've been pie-eyed over this girl for months, and after seeing her at court today, it's plain as spring water she's just as pie-eyed over you."

Emily flushed, wondering if it were possible to feel any worse. "Miss Bancroft—"

The older woman shushed her. "I've come up with the perfect solution," she announced, bracing her gnarled hands on the arms of the chair and leaning forward. "I've gotten too old for Connecticut winters, and although I can't say I'm overly fond of the South—such dreadful humidity!—I must confess it's likely to be easier on these arthritic old bones. I plan to move into," she paused, shooting Emily a shrewd, calculating glance, "into *my* house, and it will become my winter residence. Emily will remain living there until the two of you marry—I'm getting too old to live alone anyway. After the wedding Simon can either find me an acceptable cottage nearby, or have one built."

She lifted her chin to an imperious angle and regarded the two stunned individuals before her. "The house will be my wedding present to you both. Well? Are you both agreeable to that?" She examined Emily closely a minute. "I admit to being somewhat set in my ways, and I can't abide laziness and stupidity. But I daresay we'll get along fairly well—you're a teacher by profession, I understand."

"Yes, ma'am." Emily found her way to a worn wingback sofa and sat down. "But you hate me...." She shook her head in bewilderment. "I took your house away...."

Iris hooted in derision. "Balderdash! I was mad, girl, but I'd never met you. How could I hate you? The past few weeks, if you must know, I've reluctantly had to accept the fact that I maintain a grudging respect for you."

She marked Simon with an old-fashioned look. "Anyone who can catch and keep this footloose young devil has to have something besides a pretty face." She lifted her cane and pointed it at Emily. "You hide the looks you have, but it didn't fool me. And it obviously hasn't fooled my grandnephew. Well, Emily Carson? Is it a deal?"

Emily looked at Simon, who had started grinning, a wide grin that spread from ear to ear. She looked at Iris, whose stern, glacial demeanor was dissolving into wrinkles and twinkles right before Emily's disbelieving eyes. She looked down at her lap, trying to comprehend what was happening. *Dear God,* she found herself pleading silently, *what do I do now?* The cold, choking panic spread, freezing her veins. Her heart.

She couldn't trust these people. She couldn't. One day they would decide she wasn't worth their while and would leave her stranded and alone again. "It won't work," she said, her voice small but set. "I can't do it."

Simon's grin faded and his green eyes narrowed to slits. "What do you mean by that?" he questioned, very softly. Iris's back stiffened, but she held her tongue.

Emily made a short, jerking gesture with her arm. "I can't marry you."

"You love me, Emily. You can deny it until the cows come home, but you love me as much as I love you. If you'd stop being so blasted defensive and prickly, you'd admit I feel about as much pity for you as I do the characters who hauled you off in a gunny sack." His nostrils flared when Emily shook her head. "I'm not above trying a little kidnapping of my own."

"Leave the girl alone," interrupted Iris sharply, surprisingly. "She's been through enough and doesn't need your bullying and browbeating."

A long, painfully tense moment followed. Simon measured both the truth of his great-aunt's words—and Emily's infuriating mind-set. Throat tight, a muscle twitching in his cheek, he faced Emily down until she turned her head away.

A childhood memory came to Simon suddenly, wrenchingly: He'd caught a fledgling blue jay and wanted to keep it for a pet in the new birdhouse he'd just built. To make sure the bird didn't escape, he held it tightly in both hands and ran all the way home.

Excited, breathless, he called for his brother and sister, but when he carefully opened his hands to show them the bird, it was dead.

"I only wanted to keep it safe and give it a home," he'd sobbed to his father.

Dad laid a comforting hand on his shoulder. "Son, sometimes the best way to help a fledgling bird is to just let it go, so it can learn to fly on its own."

"All right," Simon said now, his voice raw because he couldn't hide the pain. "All right, Emily. I'll leave you alone, give you some time." He reached out and brushed a tear from her cheek with trembling fingers. "But try not to take too long, sparrow-girl. I'm not as strong as you think."

They arrived back at the house a little before five o'clock. Simon muttered something about working in his portable office a little while. He shot Emily a brief glance and disappeared inside the camper.

The sultry day was finally cooling from a tentative afternoon breeze. Emily changed into some light cotton slacks and a three-quarter raglan sleeve pullover, then wandered around the house like a displaced ghost. Pausing in front of the stained glass window in the library, her fingers gently traced along a dust-covered fragment molded into the likeness of a flower. Someday it would be a rich sunset hue...but she wouldn't be here to see it.

She meandered out onto the front porch, moodily scanning the burned field behind the house. Though still charred and blackened, nature was already healing the wound, covering the area with weeds and autumn wildflowers. Somewhere in the woods came the faint, far-off sound of a dog barking.

A dog? When this house was the only property for two miles in every direction? The faint sound echoed again. Emily froze, not moving, not breathing, her entire body straining to hear.

There! Over in the direction of the old campsite she and Ivan had discovered. Was it possible that they hadn't killed him? Could it be? If they hadn't really killed Ivan—

Even as her brain formulated the thought, her feet were in motion, flying down the steps and across the yard. "Ivan!" she screamed with every ounce of breath in her body. "Ivan! Where are you?"

From behind she vaguely registered Simon's voice shouting her name, telling her to wait, to stay away from the woods. She ignored him. Didn't he understand? She had to find out, *had* to see if she had heard a dog and if it had been Ivan.

She no more thought about drug rings or nefarious criminals or what had happened the last time she strayed into these woods than she heeded Simon's frantic yells for her to come back. Heart in her throat, she ran all the way across the field and plunged into the woods, calling Ivan's name as she fought her way through the underbrush.

She was halfway down the old logging road before Simon caught up with her. He snagged her shoulder, jerked her around, and held on grimly as she fought to free herself. Sobbing, pummeling, kicking, she finally managed to wrench loose. "I have to see!" she cried frantically. "Simon, I heard a dog bark—it might be Ivan. I have to see!"

"Emily—honey, it's too dangerous. It's almost dark, and the woods are probably full of stray dogs." He advanced upon her cautiously, keeping his voice low and reasonable. "Come on, now. Let's go back to the house. You know you don't need to be out in these woods until the police—"

"I don't care!" she flung back. Her hair had tumbled out of its neat bun and spilled about her face and neck and down her back. Emily swiped at it, then turned away. "I have to find out!" she repeated, her voice breaking. She ran off, down the trail, with Simon at her heels.

Moments later she burst into a clearing, lungs on fire, eyes blurred with tears so that for a moment she had no awareness beyond her furiously pounding heart. Then Simon was there, his arm going about her shoulders and holding her to him in a bone-crunching hug.

"You don't listen too good, Ms. Carson," a gravelly voice chided from just behind her. "And now we got ourselves a problem."

sixteen

It was two hours later, more or less. Though Emily knew it must be dark outside, with a blindfold covering her eyes, her mouth gagged, and her hands tied behind her back, her only certainty was the knowledge that she and Simon were still alive.

The van in which they'd been traveling had stopped. With cautious, surreptitious movements she wriggled her body, trying to loosen stiff, numbed muscles. Trying, less successfully, not to worry about Simon.

She couldn't hear anything but the sound of her own harsh, raspy breathing. Was he conscious yet? She remembered seeing two men coming toward them, remembered Simon trying to thrust her out of the way. Her frightened gaze caught a blur of movement and she had tried to call out to Simon.

She was too slow, too late. Something hard struck the back of his head, and the arm holding her had dropped away.

Emily had gone a little crazy then, but recalled little except Gumshoe yelling hoarsely for them to either tie her up and gag her, or he'd take care of her the same way. Before the pimply-faced young man and swarthy looking Latin-type had succeeded, Emily managed to scratch deep furrows across the young man's cheek, and the other guy would wear bruises on his shins for days.

Suffocating terror roared back through her. Emily choked back a sob, repeating in her mind like a litany: They weren't dead yet. The probability nonetheless loomed before her like a mushroom cloud, and so, ever since they had been tossed into the back of what felt like a stripped to the bones van, Emily had been praying.

She prayed because she had no other hope, because Simon was unable to do so, and until he had groaned and moved awhile ago, she hadn't even been certain he *was* alive. She must *not* think about the feelings she had endured then.

In her head, she sang all the songs she had learned in choir over the years, and whenever the fear threatened to choke her and send her back into a nether world of screaming phantoms and leering demons, she thought of sparrows and all the verses Simon had quoted with such deep faith over the past months.

Simon...Simon, please be all right. Lord, please let Simon be all right. Help us, please. Give me the strength to endure...God, please let me know You are there.

No legions of angels descended to set them free, and no fiery chariots swept down to burn their unsavory abductors to a crisp. But a small, steady voice had surfaced from the deepest part of her being. *I'll never change. You'll always have Me, and I will always be with you, my child. Just like salvation—My love is forever.*

Emily hung on to that Voice—and waited.

The van doors opened with a screeching jerk. Ungentle hands hauled them out, and a minute later she was unceremoniously dumped onto some sort of hard floor.

"Tie 'em both good," a voice grunted nearby. "And make sure this shack burns long enough to destroy any evidence."

"Alright, alright...whadaya think I am—a dummy? And I know it has to look like an accident, right?" That was the young, pimply-faced man, the one who promised Ivan had been taken care of.

Heart racing, Emily struggled impotently against the bonds. This couldn't be happening, it wasn't real—

"Hurry it up, you two! I want to get outta here." Emily felt a rough rope passed around her middle, then her back was against Simon's and she realized they were being tied together. Bile rose in her throat, and in spite of the last hours of steadfast prayer, a strangled sob escaped.

Incredibly, she felt the muscles in Simon's back constrict, press harder against her, and his elbows, locked with the rope to hers, moved with the slightest of gestures. He was conscious! He was even aware of what was going on and was trying to reassure her.

Confidence and renewed determination flooded through Emily, spilling new life into her numb limbs and floundering heart. She couldn't see, she was afraid to try and speak, she could barely move—but now she could hope. *Thank you, Lord! Oh, thank you! Now please get us out of here.*

The smell of burning wood and sound of crackling flames jarred Emily momentarily out of her euphoria. She began to struggle convulsively until the urgent pressure of Simon's back and arms once again calmed her.

"That'll do it. Now let's split." A harsh guttural laugh grated their ears. "So long, lovebirds. You won't be gettin' in the way anymore, will you?"

A door slammed, and they were alone with the gathering strength of the fire radiating heat and terror.

The minute the door shut, Simon began speaking. His words were barely legible, hard to hear over the fire, and Emily realized he'd been gagged as well. But she responded to his voice like a morning glory to the sun.

"Prss magain' muh back," he ordered, and she understood immediately what he was trying to do. It had been a game growing up—sitting back to back and seeing if you could stand up without using your arms. Little did she suspect then how useful such a game could be. Without hesitation she matched the pressure against her back, bent her knees, and as she felt Simon rising, tried to counter with a similar move.

"Muh ft..." she croaked, tumbling sideways because her ankles were bound. After a heart-stopping moment, she managed to regain her balance, and they stayed upright.

For another moment they stood motionless, recovering breath and gathering wits. "Jus' relak. Truh to jus' come wif me," Simon managed, the crackling flames and growing smoke fumes rendering comprehension almost impossible.

He seemed to be trying to edge in the direction of where they had heard the door slam, and it took only one step for Emily to realize they hadn't bound his feet like they had hers, probably because he had been unconscious at the time.

Simon seemed to realize about the same time that hers *were* bound, since she had had to hop instead of step. He moderated his step so she could hop without falling. Sweat poured down her body, soaking into her clothes, and she couldn't seem to stop the tremors in her arms and legs. But she stayed upright, close to Simon, and hopped.

Behind them the fire roared as it engulfed something even more flammable. Suddenly Simon ran into the wall, and she heard his muffled groan. Tears sprang to Emily's eyes. This was her fault. Simon was hurt, and might die—and it was her fault, just like Ivan's death had been her fault.

Simon turned so that their hands could just touch the coarse, unfinished boards that made up the walls of the shack, already hot to the touch. Choking, gagging, Emily prayed.

Then she heard the doorknob rattle, and her bound wrists twisted along with Simon's as he struggled to turn the knob and open the door. When she felt it opening and pushing her almost off balance again, she sobbed against the restraining gag, feeling the inrush of cool air against her face, in her hair.

Simon did not waste time trying to talk anymore. Instead, he encouraged her through a series of firm but urgent tugs to follow him. As they jerked and hopped out the mercifully unlocked door, the sound of crashing wood exploded behind them and part of the ceiling collapsed.

With a sucking roar of redoubled intensity, the triumphant fire devoured the interior of the shack. Emily felt the heat of it blasting her, searing her as Simon all but dragged her on his back the last few feet.

They were still too close to the burning structure when she lost her balance again and tumbled sideways, throwing Simon off-balance too so that they both fell to the ground. She heard him grunt in pain, and frantically struggled to get back up with him before he passed out. Too close—they were too close to the shack, and the flames and heat could still accomplish their deadly mission. And it was her fault.

Once again the firm, steady pressure of Simon's back

quieted her, guided her. "Easy, love," she thought he said, and in mere seconds they managed to regain their feet. With herculean effort, Emily managed to keep from panicking again, blindly obeying the largely unspoken communication of the man to whom she was literally bound.

The analogy burst into her soul like the consuming brightness of flame: She was trusting this man with her life, not knowing where he was going, and she was unable to either see him or give him much aid on her own. He wasn't leaving her behind because it was her fault, or trying to make her feel guilty. He was only working to save her life.

And *that* was the way she should trust God, whom she could neither see nor hear. Nor did she know exactly where He was leading her. She certainly couldn't offer Him much aid on her own. All she could do was surrender, no longer resisting.

Just as she knew Simon would give his life to keep her from all harm, was struggling to do that right now—so she realized, truly understood for the first time in her life, how much God cared for her. Cared for her so much that He sent His beloved Son to die for her, even though the fault was hers—not His.

She, Emily Carson, did matter after all. And there *was* Someone who loved her...who had always loved her. Loved her as she yearned to be loved. *Oh, Lord, she prayed in everlasting gratitude, thank You. Thank You for restoring the joy of my salvation—thanks for Your faithfulness in spite of me!*

After awhile she came to the more fundamental awareness that Simon was fumbling with the cords that bound their wrists. For several frustrating minutes he worked in silence, but it was no use. He muttered something unintelligible. "Muh fingehs...too big...."

Emily moved her raw, throbbing wrists back together and found his fingers with her own. She pressed, trying to tell him to let her try. His fingers brushed against her wrists and jerked, and Emily knew he was probably feeling the rawness and seeping blood.

"Ahm okay." She gagged again, so quit trying to talk, focusing every atom of her concentration on working the knots in the slender cords free. Her back and shoulders burned, and behind them she could hear the snapping, crackling flames, smell the charred wood and choking smoke.

"Oo can do it. Take ur time. 'At's it." Simon coached her, soothed her, encouraged her as if they had all the time in the world.

I can do it, Emily ground out to herself. *I've done it before*. This was no different from the time J.J. and his stupid little friends tied her up when she was eleven and left her in the woods. She escaped then, and she could do it again.

This was no different, yet it was. Then, she'd been alone. Now Simon was with her. And not only Simon, she thought with growing excitement. *I can do it, because You're with me,* she prayed. *With Christ I can do all things.*

A minute later she succeeded in loosening the knot, and with a violent tug, Simon came free of the bonds. He worked with savage speed to untie the rope that bound him and Emily together.

"Almost home free, love," he enunciated clearly,

directly in her ear, and Emily knew then they would be. He twisted and dropped a kiss on the top of her head as he swiftly untied the gag and tugged off her blindfold.

Two minutes later they were both free, and fell into each other's arms.

They were sitting beneath a pine tree, for Emily's legs had given out, and Simon was running his hands over her the same way she was doing him. "It takes more than a knock or two to keep me down," he consoled her with a white-toothed grin, barely visible in the flickering light of the fire. "I'm okay, honey. Stop shaking now—I'm okay." He laughed a little. "I'm more worried about you than you are me, so how about if you reassure me for a minute?"

"I'm fine—just sore, mostly on my wrist where it was cut. And my jaws and shoulders hurt."

He lifted her wrists and rubbed his thumbs gently over the raw, blistered skin, then tilted the bandaged one up toward the fire to try and examine it better. The thick gauze bandage she had taped there that morning was crumpled, but at least it had been thick enough to protect the wound.

"What about the fire?" Emily asked, and they both turned to gaze at the remainder of the shack.

"It looks like it's just going to burn itself out, fortunately."

Even as he spoke, the two remaining walls toppled into the center of the fire, sending an explosion of sparks and flames shooting into the night. The building had been placed in a clearing, so there were no trees or even protruding branches close enough for the fire to refuel itself with and roar into new life.

Simon put his arm around Emily, and she dropped her head onto his shoulder. They sat beneath the pine and watched until the flames died, first to flickering tongues, then to a glowing pile of embers and a wavering column of smoke.

"We were supposed to be in there," Emily spoke at last into the night, and a spasm shuddered through her weary frame.

Simon hugged her harder. "I know," he agreed quietly. "But we weren't." He cupped her face and kissed her very tenderly. "Let's thank God for our lives, then see about finding shelter for the night."

They bowed their heads, and Simon offered an eloquent prayer of thankfulness that melted Emily's heart completely. How could she have been so blind not to know she was head over heels in love with this man?

She rubbed her damp cheek against his shirt, basking in the steady beating of his heart. Her fingers crept up to softly touch his beard-roughened cheek. "Simon? I've been praying—a lot—these past hours and you know what? Never has God been so real to me. I felt—really *felt*—His power and presence surrounding me, sustaining me...us. And everything you've been saying all these months suddenly made perfect sense."

Incredibly, his chest heaved, and a sob of utter relief seared her ears. Then his arms hauled her up and he kissed her, words and tears all mixing up together. Emily eventually managed to wriggle a hand between to cover his mouth.

"You haven't let me tell you something else," she laughed, breathless, her own eyes aching with tears of joy.

"What's that?"

"I love you with all my heart, Simon Balfour...and if you still want to marry a plain brown sparrow who doesn't feel insignificant anymore...she's yours."

"Oh, God, *thank* You!" Simon vowed, passion and relief making his voice shake. "Yes, yes, yes, you impossible woman—of course I still want to marry you."

"Even though I almost killed us both?"

He kissed her. "Hush. I love all of you, Emily Carson—including the impulsive, unthinking woman who has a thing for ugly animals."

Emily dug an elbow into his ribs. "Just for that—I'm only marrying you to stay in the house!"

Simon grabbed a fistful of her hair and wrapped it around her throat. "That was *my* line, remember?"

Emily pulled his head down, and for the next few minutes neither of them said anything. Eventually Simon lifted his head, his fingers smoothing her face. Cradled in his arms, surrounded by enveloping darkness, Emily knew she had found a home at last.

"Simon?"

"Hmm?"

"Let's make sure we clean the window before the wedding, okay?"

"No-o problem."

Epilogue

The day after Thanksgiving, Emily, Simon, and Aunt Iris were sitting on the front porch, rocking in three of the huge wicker rockers Simon bought from the couple in South Carolina whose old country inn he would be restoring after Christmas. The sun had finally broken through the storm clouds which had dumped an inch of rain Thanksgiving day.

Emily rocked in blissful contentment, holding her husband's hand and watching the sunbeams streaming down into the dripping yard. "It was nice of Sheriff Jessup to phone the good news yesterday, even though it was Thanksgiving," she mused dreamily. Simon squeezed her hand.

"It took him long enough to pass it on," Iris observed. "Almost had to serve stone-cold turkey." She chuckled. "But I must admit I enjoyed the meal a lot more, knowing they finally caught all those despicable men and locked them up tight."

"Without bail," Simon added. "All of them, including Gumshoe." His gaze moved lovingly over Emily, causing her to blush. "God sure moves in mysterious ways—using a murdering drug dealer to finally convince my wife," he leaned over and kissed Emily, "that she couldn't live without me—or the Lord."

Iris snorted. "If you two are going to start acting like a pair of billing and cooing doves again, I'm going back inside."

Simon chuckled and stood. "Don't move. Emily and I will go for a walk."

"Simon—it's too wet."

He ignored her laughing protests and hauled her into his arms, carrying her. "There. Quit complaining, sparrow-girl. I want to watch the sun shining on our window."

"Oh." Emily relaxed, hugging him. "In that case...."

He carried her out into the yard, finding just the right spot to best savor their pride and joy.

"I like the purple iris best," Emily announced after a few minutes of rapt contemplation. "It's incredible the way the sun makes all the colors so rich and alive—Simon? What is it?"

He had cocked his head in a listening stance, turning his face to the field behind the house. He wasn't even looking at the window. In exasperation Emily twisted her head. "What are you doing?"

"I thought I saw—" he stopped, then gently set Emily down. "Yes. There, near the edge of the field. Something moved."

"Probably a rabbit."

"Nope, too big. Didn't you say you'd seen some deer—" his voice died, the hand loosely clasping Emily's waist suddenly jerking her hard against him.

Emily peered across the field, and then she heard it: a weak but very definite "woof." And saw, very briefly, a large bony head. "Ivan...."

They tore off across the field, oblivious to the wet scratchy weeds and soggy earth, coming to a breathless halt to stare in disbelief at the animal whining weakly at their feet. Dropping to her knees, Emily gathered the gaunt, filthy dog into her arms, sobbing. "Ivan, Ivan.... You're alive!" Ivan's bullwhip tail thumped weakly.

Simon was shaking his head. "I don't suppose we'll ever know what the old boy endured—or why they didn't kill him instead of dumping him somewhere. It's probably taken him all this time to find his way home."

Emily looked across at him, eyes swimming in tears. "He came home," she repeated, so choked with happiness and tears she could barely speak.

Simon grinned. "Well, I guess I'll have to change my way of thinking about ugly smelly dogs now, won't I?" He knelt, his hand coming down to join Emily's, stroking Ivan's floppy ears and filthy head. Then he gently elbowed Emily aside and lifted the dog into his arms. Ivan licked his face feebly—and Simon didn't even grimace. "Come on, you ugly, overgrown moose," he said, "let's go home."

And they made their way back across the field, to the welcoming, beckoning house.

A Letter To Our Readers

Dear Readers:

In order that we might better contribute to your reading enjoyment, we would appreciate your taking a few minutes to respond to the following questions and return to:

Editor
Heartsong Presents
P.O. Box 719
Uhrichsville, Ohio 44683

1. Did you enjoy reading *Restore the Joy*?
   - ❑ Very much. I would like to see more books by this author!
   - ❑ Moderately
   - ❑ I would have enjoyed it more if

   ____

2. Where did you purchase this book? __________

   ____

3. What influenced your decision to purchase this book?

❑ Cover	❑ Back cover copy
❑ Title	❑ Friends
❑ Publicity	❑ Other __________

4. Please rate the following elements from 1 (poor) to 10 (superior).
   - ❑ Heroine
   - ❑ Plot
   - ❑ Hero
   - ❑ Inspirational theme
   - ❑ Setting
   - ❑ Secondary characters

5. What settings would you like to see in Heartsong Presents Books?

   ____

   ____

6. What are some inspirational themes you would like to see treated in future books?

   ____

   ____

7. Would you be interested in reading other Heartsong Presents books?
   - ❑ Very interested
   - ❑ Moderately interested
   - ❑ Not interested

8. Please indicate your age:
   - ❑ Under 18
   - ❑ 25-34
   - ❑ 46-55
   - ❑ 18-24
   - ❑ 35-45
   - ❑ Over 55

Name ______________________________________

Occupation ______________________________________

Address ______________________________________

City ____________________ State ________ Zip ____________